MW00790600

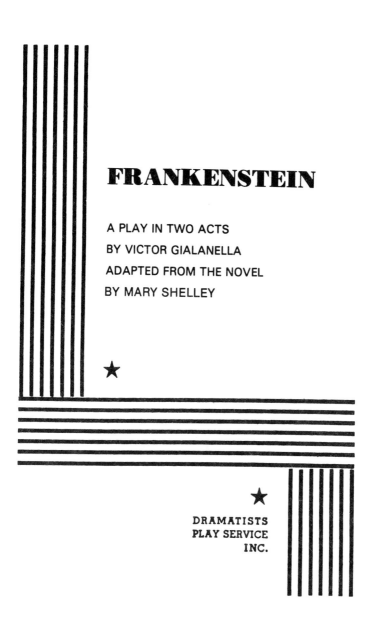

FRANKENSTEIN

A PLAY IN TWO ACTS
BY VICTOR GIALANELLA
ADAPTED FROM THE NOVEL
BY MARY SHELLEY

★

★

DRAMATISTS
PLAY SERVICE
INC.

FRANKENSTEIN was presented by Terry Allen Kramer, Joseph Kipness, James M. Nederlander and Stewart F. Lane, in association with Twentieth-Century Fox Productions, at the Palace Theatre, in New York City, on January 4, 1981. It was directed by Tom Moore; the scenery was designed by Douglas W. Schmidt; the special effects and sound were designed by Bran Ferren; the costumes were designed and puppets conceived by Carrie F. Robbins; the lighting was designed by Jules Fisher and Robby Monk; and the music was by Richard Peaslee. The cast, in order of appearance, was as follows:

VICTOR FRANKENSTEIN .... David Dukes

HANS METZ .... John Seitz

PETER SCHMIDT .... Dennis Bacigalupi

HENRY CLERVAL .... John Glover

ELIZABETH LAVENZA .... Dianne Wiest

WILLIAM FRANKENSTEIN .... Scott Schwartz

JUSTINE MORITZ .... Jill P. Rose

LIONEL MUELLER...................... Richard Kneeland

FRAU MUELLER .... Kate Wilkinson

ALPHONSE FRANKENSTEIN .... Douglas Seale

THE CREATURE .... Keith Jochim

DE LACEY .... John Carradine

FRANKENSTEIN was first presented at the Loretto-Hilton Repertory Theatre, in St. Louis, Missouri, in March, 1979.

CAST OF CHARACTERS

VICTOR FRANKENSTEIN . . . . A Young Scientist
ELIZABETH LAVENZA . . . . His adopted "Cousin"
ALPHONSE FRANKENSTEIN . . . . His Father
WILLIAM FRANKENSTEIN . . . . His Younger Brother

HENRY CLERVAL . . . . A Friend of Victor's
LIONEL MUELLER . . . . The Local Magistrate
FRAU MUELLER . . . . His Wife
HANS METZ . . . . A Villager
PETER SCHMIDT . . . . A Villager
DELACEY . . . . A Blind Hermit
JUSTINE MORITZ . . . . A Maidservant

THE CREATURE

The action of the play takes place in and around the Frankenstein Estate, Geneva, Switzerland, in the mid-1800's.

ACT I

ACT II

"Did I request thee, Maker, from my clay
To mould me Man, did I solicit thee
From darkness to promote me?"

— Paradise Lost, X, 743-45

(*Music 1.*)
(*MUSIC 1a.*)   ACT I

PROLOGUE
Bleak, white, endless space. A raging snowstorm projected onto
scrim. The sound of fiercely howling wind.
Victor Frankenstein appears D.L., *only his head and shoulders*
visible in a cold, blue light.

VICTOR. I, Victor Frankenstein, am damned. My crimes will
be recorded here so that all may know of the unending horror I
have wrought. It is through this means that I give warning lest
someone else be tempted to explore this most unholy path.
Father, I have left instructions for this journal to be sent to you
only after I am dead. It is fitting in a way that you should be the
first to hear my tale. The Demon has survived. (*Two figures ap-*
pear in the distance. The one in front is considerably larger than the other.
Slowly, they move across the space.) Many months have passed since
that dreadful night of terror, but he still remains before me,
mocking me and beckoning me to follow. We are fueled by the
passions of our mutual hate and he leads me daily farther and
farther into the everlasting ices of the north. We are in a region
uninhabited by man and I know that he has brought me here to
share his loneliness and isolation; but the emptiness and bitter
cold are fitting complement to my moral resolution. I am
responsible for everything that he has done and cannot rest until he is destroyed. For He is my Creation; and while he yet remains alive, I shall remain forever cursed. (*The figures*
disappear.) Read now, Father, of all that I have done. Do not
bother to condemn me, for like the Titan who aspired to om-
nipotence, I am already chained in an eternal hell...

Blackout (*MUSIC 2.*)

6

FRANKENSTEIN

ACT I

Scene I

A Graveyard. Evening.
Shrouded by fog, we can barely make out the facade of a church.
There is a crumbling stone wall with a gate running offstage. A
few crooked, aging tombstones stand about, leaves clustered
around their bases, held there by a softly moaning wind. There
is an open grave, a pick and shovel lying on the ground next to
it.
(MUSIC 2a.) Slowly, a corpse is pushed up and out of the
grave, followed by Hans Metz, a villager. He pulls the body a
little distance away. Peter Schmidt, another villager, emerges
with a lantern. They crouch next to the body.
Victor enters with a lantern.

VICTOR. What's taking you so long?
METZ. We didn't want to damage him, sir.
SCHMIDT. No, sir. We were being very careful, sir.
VICTOR. Yes. I'm sure. How did this one die?
SCHMIDT. He was hanged, sir.
VICTOR. Hanged?
METZ. Yes, sir. Just a few hours ago.
VICTOR. Then the neck is broken and he is useless to me.
METZ. No. sir.
VICTOR. I've been very specific with you about my needs.
And once again you've done nothing more than waste my time.
(*He starts to go.*)
METZ. No, sir! See for yourself, sir. (*Victor glares at them a mo-*
ment, then moves to the body and examines it.)
SCHMIDT. Is he all right?

VICTOR. (*Pleased.*) Yes. It seems Herr Mueller has no feel for the tying of the knot.

METZ. No, sir.

VICTOR. (*Rises.*) Very well, then. Bring it just as quickly as you can. I must return to spend the evening with my family.

METZ. How nice for you, sir.

VICTOR. Yes, it is. Be careful you're not seen. Herr Mueller will be there for dinner. (*Starts to go.*)

METZ. And the money, sir?

VICTOR. It will be the same as always.

SCHMIDT. But, sir. This one is so fresh. And healthy.

VICTOR. What you're doing hardly qualifies you to make demands.

METZ. But it would appear, sir, that you must meet them. (*There is the sound of a carriage approaching.*)

VICTOR. I can't risk being seen. (*The carriage appears behind the wall, stops.*)

METZ. We'll take care of you, sir. If you'll take care of us.

VICTOR. Leave it in the usual place. The money will be waiting. (*He exits. The carriage door opens.*)

METZ. Quickly. Hide. Over there.

HENRY. (*Off.*) Hello? (*They scramble into position with the shovel and pick. The gate opens. Henry Clerval enters. He is in his late 20's. Proper. Articulate. A Gentleman.*) Hello? Anyone here?

METZ. (*Stepping out.*) What do you want here?

HENRY. Please. Excuse me. I have come a long way. Night came upon us and my driver found himself lost. We saw your light and hoped you might be able to give us some directions.

METZ. Yes. I'm working late tonight, Herr...?

HENRY. Clerval. Henry Clerval.

METZ. Herr Clerval. A convict's grave, you see? He was hanged this very day. Best to dispose of him quick, before the rot sets in.

HENRY. Yes. I am certain. (*Schmidt stumbles. Henry turns, sees him.*) You are not alone?

SCHMIDT. No, sir.

METZ. Just... the three of us, sir.

HENRY. The three of...? (*Metz chuckles, looks at body.*) Yes, I see. Please. My destination is the Chateau Frankenstein. I am already quite late. Can you...

8

SCHMIDT. The Chateau Frankenstein?

HENRY. Yes. Do you know it?

METZ. We have had occasion to go there. (*Metz and Schmidt approach slowly. There is the tension of possible violence.*)

SCHMIDT. You are a friend of the young Herr Frankenstein?

HENRY. Yes, I am. From the university at Inglestadt.

SCHMIDT. Ah!

HENRY. The Chateau? Is it nearby?

METZ. Yes. Follow the road north to Geneva for perhaps, oh, two kilometers. There is a fork to your right. Take it and you will come to the Chateau.

HENRY. Thank you. You have been of great service. (*Hands him a coin. Starts to go.*) Good night.

METZ. Herr Clerval?

HENRY. Yes?

METZ. Are you a religious man, sir?

HENRY. Why?

METZ. I thought perhaps, sir, you might say a few words before we lay him down.

HENRY. I think not.

METZ. But, sir. Should any man have to go to heaven unannounced?

HENRY. I should think the smell alone would have forewarned them of his coming.

METZ. Yes, sir.

HENRY. Good night. (*He exits. They watch as the carriage starts to drive off.*)

METZ. (*Calling.*) Good night, sir. Travel safely. (*The carriage is gone.*) That was close, Peter.

SCHMIDT. You gave him the wrong directions, Hans.

METZ. Yes. Hopefully it will delay him long enough. Now, let's finish up quickly and be gone. (*They begin to wrap the body as the lights fade.*) (*MUSIC 3.*)

ACT I

Scene 2

A sitting room of the Chateau. Later that evening.

U.C. is a double set of French doors, leading outside. They are separated by a tapestried panel containing the crest of the House of Frankenstein. U.L. are double wooden doors leading to the rest of the house. U.R. an ornate mantelpeice with a softly glowing fire. There are a sofa and table C. D.L. are two sidechairs separated by a table. Behind it an elegant sideboard set with glasses and decanters. D.R. is a matching armchair.

(MUSIC 3a.) Lights come up on Victor standing behind the sofa. Elizabeth Lavenza is seated in the armchair, reading a story to William, who sits on the floor in front of her with his dog, Fritz. Justine Moritz, a young maidservant, sits embroidering in the D.L. sidechair.

ELIZABETH. (*Reads.*) ...The day was fast approaching when the queen would have to keep her bargain with the monstrous little man and deliver to him her first born child in exchange for the secret of spinning straw into gold that he had given her. Her only hope was to learn the little monster's name.

WILLIAM. What did she do?

ELIZABETH. (*Rises.*) Well. She searched for him everywhere that she could think of and was just about to give up hope when she came upon a little house in the woods and saw the horrible little man singing and dancing around a fire. (*Justine jumps up and assumes the character of the little man.*)

JUSTINE. Today I bake and tomorrow brew my beer
The day after that the queen's child shall be here
How lucky it 'tis that no one knows
My name is...

WILLIAM. Rumpulstiltskin!

JUSTINE. Ho, Ho!

ELIZABETH. Well, you can imagine how delighted she was when she heard the name. So, the next day, when the little monster finally appeared at the castle, at first she asked: "Is your name Thomas?"

WILLIAM AND JUSTINE. "No."

ELIZABETH. "Is your name... (*A look.*) ... Victor?"

WILLIAM AND JUSTINE. "No."

ELIZABETH. "Is it, perchance..."

WILLIAM. "Rumpulstiltskin!"

JUSTINE. "The devil told you that! The devil told you that!"

ELIZABETH. And in his rage he stamped his foot so hard that he sank into the ground up to his waist. Then he siezed his other leg and tore himself asunder in the middle. (*Justine attempts to pantomime this and succeeds only in causing herself to fall, much to the delight of the others.*) Oh, Justine!

WILLIAM. Victor?

VICTOR. Yes, William?

WILLIAM. What does as-under mean?

VICTOR. Asunder. It means he tore himself in half.

WILLIAM. Oh. Why did he do that?

JUSTINE. Because he was angry about not getting what he wanted. (*Justine picks up Fritz and places him on Elizabeth's lap.*)

ELIZABETH. Do you understand?

WILLIAM. Yes. I think so.

VICTOR. (*Lifting him up.*) Good. Off you go now.

JUSTINE. It's time for your bath.

WILLIAM. Ohhhh!

VICTOR. Here now, little brother. None of that. You know what happens to little boys who won't take their baths, don't you?

WILLIAM. What?

VICTOR. (*Crouching, he extends his arms, his hands twisted, and approaches slowly. Willian's eyes go wide and he backs away.*) Goblins and vampires rise up in the middle of the night...

ELIZABETH. Victor!

VICTOR. They reach out slowly and then they... (*He grabs him and lifts him into the air, tickles him. William squirms, laughs.*)... grab you up and carry you away!

ELIZABETH. (*Laughing with them.*) Victor! Leave him alone! Victor!

VICTOR. All right. (*He sets him down.*) Off with you now. Go on.

WILLIAM. There are no such things as monsters.

ELIZABETH. No. Of course there aren't.

JUSTINE. Come along, love.

WILLIAM. Come on, Fritz. (*Elizabeth hands him his dog.*)

ELIZABETH. I shall be up to hear your prayers and tuck you in. (*They start out.*)

JUSTINE. We'll go up and check for monsters. (*They are gone, Justine shutting the door behind them.*)

ELIZABETH. How wonderful it's been to have had you with us here tonight. You've been so abstracted and removed of late.

VICTOR. I've just been in my workshop.

ELIZABETH. Yes. But for all that we have seen of you you may as well have been in Inglestadt. Is your work so secretive that it can't be shared with us?

VICTOR. (*Teasing.*) I will share one thing with you: My work would take me half the time if it weren't for you.

ELIZABETH. Me? And why is that?

VICTOR. Easily half the time I find myself staring thoughtlessly into space, thinking of you, seeing your face, longing for your touch. I would come and find you but for the fact that my work does keep me very busy.

ELIZABETH. You are hardly busy now.

VICTOR. No. I most certainly am not. (*They draw together slowly and kiss. After a moment, Lionel Mueller, the local magistrate, opens the door and enters the room.*)

MUELLER. Ah, here you are. (*Calling off.*) Here they are. Found them in the parlour. (*To them.*) And none too soon, from the looks of things, eh? (*Crossing to Elizabeth.*) William off to bed?

ELIZABETH. Yes. Justine is just seeing to his...

MUELLER. Wonderful boy. Doing quite a good job with him, my dear. Quite a good job. His mother, rest her soul, would be well pleased.

ELIZABETH. Thank you, Herr Mueller. William makes it...

MUELLER. She had the greatest expectations when she first brought you into the family. And I'm pleased to say that you've surpassed them all. Eh, Victor?

VICTOR. Yes. I think that she has more than...

MUELLER. (*Crossing back to the door.*) Where the devil are they? They were right behind me when I left the dining room.

12

(*Victor and Elizabeth cross to each other and try to steal a kiss. Mueller turns, catches them.*) Ah, ah, ah! Here they come now. (*Calling out.*) Thought you might have tried to get away from me. You know what they say about old friends and beautiful wives.

FRAU M. (*Entering.*) Oh, Lionel! Behave yourself. The very thought that I would ever dream of such a thing...

MUELLER. Yes, yes.

ALPHONSE. (*Entering.*) Victor. We have a surprise for you.

VICTOR. What is it, father? (*Alphonse turns to the door. Henry enters, presents himself with a flourish.*) Henry!

HENRY. Victor! (*They embrace.*)

VICTOR. Whatever are you doing here?

HENRY. (*A joke.*) I was simply passing by and...

VICTOR. Yes, of course you were. My, but it is good to see you again.

HENRY. And you, my friend. And you. It has been much too long.

ELIZABETH. Henry.

HENRY. (*Going to her.*) Elizabeth. The beautiful Elizabeth. It's been much too long since I have seen you, too.

ELIZABETH. Yes. I have much to tell you, Henry. So many things have happened since last I wrote to you. (*Henry squeezes her hands.*)

VICTOR. (*Crossing in.*) Yes indeed, Henry. There is much I want to tell you too. My, but it is good to see you again.

ALPHONSE. Herr Clerval said that you were not expecting him.

VICTOR. No. No, I was not. Henry, what the devil are you doing here? (*Henry and Elizabeth exchange a look.*)

HENRY. (*Stammers.*) Well, I... ah...

ELIZABETH. (*Covering.*) You see how it is? We finally manage to persuade him away from his work for even a single night when even stronger competition arrives.

HENRY. Competition, indeed. There were times at school when it was all we could do to stop his unrelenting ravings on your behalf.

ELIZABETH. You embarrass me, sir.

VICTOR. Ravings, indeed. I hardly spoke of you, Elizabeth.

FRAU M. Oh, Victor. Does that mean you never spoke about Elizabeth? You should be ashamed.

13

VICTOR. Well, occasionally. (*Frau M. titters.*) That is to say, often enough. (*This is, of course, to Frau Mueller, even worse.*)

MUELLER. Give in, Victor. You only bind yourself more tightly with each and every word. (*Victor smiles, reaches down and takes Elizabeth's hand.*)

ALPHONSE. Frau Mueller, may I offer you a little sherry?

FRAU M. Yes, thank you.

ALPHONSE. Lionel. Some brandy?

MUELLER. Please. Excellent dinner by the way, Alphonse. Wasn't it, my dear?

FRAU M. Yes. Very good. I thought the leg of lamb, especially, was excellent, though I thought that the potatoes could have used a bit more...

ALPHONSE. (*Handing her the sherry.*) Thank you.

FRAU M. Thank you. (*Throughout the following, Alphonse pours and serves the others.*)

ELIZABETH. I hope you didn't mind us leaving before you'd finished, but we had promised William a story.

FRAU M. No, of course not. I only wish that I had joined you, for when these two begin to chatter, they...

MUELLER. Alphonse and I chatter? Nonsense. We were discussing the man we had to hang this afternoon. (*There is a distant rumble of thunder, the beginning of a storm which continues to build throughout the rest of the scene.*) Buried him just before coming here to dinner.

HENRY. You buried him this afternoon, Herr Mueller?

MUELLER. Yes, that's correct. Immediately after we had cut him down. It was a funny thing: the knot had worked itself loose, so instead of his neck snapping cleanly as it should have done, the poor beggar wound up slowly choking to death on his own tongue.

FRAU M. Lionel, please! We can do without these grisly details!

VICTOR. You tied the knot yourself, Herr Mueller?

MUELLER. Yes, as a matter of fact, I did. Placed it firmly just below the skull. I...

FRAU M. Lionel! Victor! Please!

MUELLER. What? Oh, yes. Sorry, my dear. (*Henry stares quizzically at Victor.*)

ALPHONSE. Herr Clerval, you have arrived, you know, at a

14

most fortuitous time. (*Henry and the Muellers look at him.*) Frau Mueller, Lionel. I have asked you here tonight to be the first to know what everyone has long suspected: that Victor and Elizabeth are to be married. (*Everyone bustles about in a flurry of congratulations.*)

HENRY. Much happiness, Elizabeth.

MUELLER. Congratulations, the both of you!

FRAU M. Oh, my dears, I am so glad that you have finally decided.

ELIZABETH. Thank you.

FRAU M. You must set a date, my dear. And you mustn't wait too long. Do not allow him time to change his mind.

MUELLER. A toast! A toast to:

The House of Frankenstein;

The great joy of it's father;

The loving memory of it's mother;

The happiness of it's children;

The bright promise of it's future;

The House of Frankenstein!

(*There is a crack of thunder and a flash of lightning. Shadows can be seen outside the U.R. French doors. Frau Mueller screams. Everyone tenses. Victor crosses to Elizabeth. The figures move toward L. Mueller crosses to the U.L. set of doors. There is another flash of lightning as he pulls them open, revealing Metz and Schmidt, who stand there stunned.*) What are you doing there?

SCHMIDT. Nothing, sir. That is, we...

MUELLER. What have you got out there?

METZ. (*Coming in.*) We have business with Herr Victor. (*To Victor.*) Isn't that right, sir?

VICTOR. ...Yes. I... I'd forgotten.

HENRY. Well, gentlemen. We meet again, eh?

MUELLER. You've met these men before, Herr Clerval?

HENRY. Yes, I have. On the road here. They... (*A look at Victor.*) . . . gave me directions to the Chateau.

METZ. Indeed we did, sir. Yes. Herr Victor, about that business?

MUELLER. Business? What business have you here at this time of night?

SCHMIDT. Something... something for Herr Frankenstein, sir.

METZ. Yes, sir. (*To Victor.*) It's concerned with something very grave.

ALPHONSE. Surely it can wait until tomorrow?

METZ. No, sir. (*To Victor.*) I don't think that it will keep that long.

MUELLER. What is it you have brought?

VICTOR. (*Irritated.*) It is certain to be of use to me, Herr Mueller. Come, gentlemen.

ALPHONSE. Victor, this is most distressing.

VICTOR. I'm sorry, father. It appears to be most urgent. I'll return shortly. Gentlemen...

METZ. Good evening all... Herr Magistrate.

SCHMIDT. ... Ladies.

HENRY. Sir. Good night. (*They exit out the French doors with Victor.*)

MUELLER. Metz and Schmidt. What have they to do with Victor?

ALPHONSE. Lord only knows. They've been here before, those two. I'm afraid that sort's the only type who'll work for him.

FRAU M. Well, the villagers think Victor a little mad, you know.

MUELLER. Now, now, my dear, there is no reason to...

ALPHONSE. No. Do not protest, my friend. I have heard the rumors.

HENRY. But, sir. What exactly is it that he's doing? (*Alphonse turns away.*)

ELIZABETH. Oh, Henry. We know nothing of the nature of his work.

HENRY. He's told you nothing?

ELIZABETH. No. That is why I wrote and asked if you would come. He has changed, Henry. He is not the man we used to know.

HENRY. When did he begin to change?

ALPHONSE. Shortly after he returned from Inglestadt. He began by transforming the tower rooms into a laboratory where he could work without "disturbance".

ELIZABETH. And then he started ordering machinery and equipment which was delivered to him at the oddest hours of the night. (*The room lights flicker once.*)

16

MUELLER. Yes. And then he hired villagers to construct that enormous wheel in the stream beneath the tower. He...

HENRY. A dynamo?

MUELLER. What?

HENRY. The wheel. It is a technique for producing... electricity. (*The lights in the room begin to flicker. There is the distant hum of electrical machinery.*)

MUELLER. What the devil's going on up there?

ALPHONSE. It's that infernal machinery of his.

HENRY. Whatever is he up to? (*Blackout.*)

ELIZABETH. As you can see, Henry, he leaves us in the dark.

ALPHONSE. I hardly find this amusing, Elizabeth. It's the very sort of thing that happens constantly. (*Lights flicker and restore.*)

FRAU M. Lionel, perhaps we should be going.

MUELLER. Yes. I think perhaps we should.

ELIZABETH. Oh, no. Please...

MUELLER. We really should be getting on. I think we may be in for quite a storm.

FRAU M. Besides, the children will be waiting up for us. Why, they just haven't the sense to go to bed, no matter how tired they may get.

MUELLER. She's right, you know. It's getting rather late.

ALPHONSE. I'm sorry that the evening should have to end like this.

MUELLER. No matter, Alphonse. It's always a pleasure to see you. Elizabeth, my dear. Much happiness.

ELIZABETH. Thank you.

MUELLER. Herr Clerval. A pleasure.

HENRY. And you, sir.

FRAU M. You come see me now, Elizabeth. You have much planning to do and I shall be only too happy to help.

ALPHONSE. Come. Let me see you out.

MUELLER. Watch out for her, my dear, or she'll take you over completely. (*They exit.*)

ELIZABETH. (*Calls.*) Goodnight!

MUELLERS. (*Off.*) (*Ad lib.*) Goodnight!

HENRY. Elizabeth, from your letter I had no idea that things were so extreme.

ELIZABETH. Oh, Henry, it gets worse with every passing

day. He will tell me nothing, but I thought that perhaps you, his closest friend, could...

HENRY. I will see to it, Elizabeth. I promise you (*Victor enters.*)

VICTOR. Is everyone gone?

HENRY. Yes. (*With calculated gaiety.*) You know, I envy you, Victor, for she is every bit the charming and delightful creature I remembered.

ELIZABETH. (*Picking up his cue.*) Herr Clerval, since you persist in embarrassing me I shall be forced to take my leave. (*To Victor.*) Besides, I promised William I would tuck him in. I am sure you will survive without me.

HENRY. How shall we survive when all the light has left the room?

ELIZABETH. There, you see? He's managed to do it again, after all. (*She kisses Victor.*) Good night. (*She starts out.*)

HENRY. Good night, dear Elizabeth. (*She turns back, a look of concern.*) And do not worry about your Victor. I promise not to keep him up too long.

ELIZABETH. I know I leave him, Henry, in the safest possible hands. Good night. (*She exits, closing the door behind her.*)

HENRY. Well, Victor?

VICTOR. Well, Henry?

HENRY. I am waiting for an explanation.

VICTOR. What do you mean?

HENRY. Those two men...

VICTOR. Now Henry, they were merely...

HENRY. Was the body very damaged?

VICTOR. (*Pause.*) No.

HENRY. Victor! What are you doing?

VICTOR. Your oath, Henry, to repeat nothing I am about to say.

HENRY. You have it.

VICTOR. Say it.

HENRY. (*Offended.*) I shall repeat nothing I am about to hear, sir! Satisfactory?

VICTOR. Please, Henry, spare me your sarcasm. You are the only one who understands my fascination with the sciences.

HENRY. Yes, yes. I am well acquainted with your interests. Please, Victor, come to the point.

VICTOR. Henry, I have reason to believe that I am capable of re-animating life.

HENRY. (*Incredulous, angry.*) This is the nature of your work? This is what consumes you? This ridiculous, age-old pursuit of eternal life?

VICTOR. No! Not eternal life, but rather the re-creation of life.

HENRY. But Victor, I...

VICTOR. Hear me out. At school I came across the works of Bolos the Egyptian, the Moslem Jabir, Albert Magnus, Roger Bacon, Paracelsus...

HENRY. Alchemists, magicians... Good God man!

VICTOR. Scientists, philosophers. Perhaps magicians. Regardless, I decided to study nature, to inquire into its secrets through its very structures. (*He sits.*) I saw how the fine form of man was wasted and degraded; I watched the corruption of death succeed to the bloom of life; I saw how the worm inherited the wonders of the eye and brain and heart. I examined and analyzed every detail of the change from life to death until, finally, I succeeded in discovering the very cause of life itself.

HENRY. Really, Victor! Do you expect me to believe such nonsense?

VICTOR. That and more. I expect you to help me in my project.

HENRY. In what way? What... project?

VICTOR. The creation of life... in a man. (*Thunder.*)

HENRY. You believe this? You actually believe this!

VICTOR. (*Rises.*) I have in my laboratory the intelligent brain of one man and the healthy heart of another, kept alive by means of induction through chemicals for well beyond a week.

HENRY. Good lord!

VICTOR. I have only been awaiting a proper vessel in which they are to be implanted. And that was just delivered to me here tonight. (*Thunder.*) The only struggle that remains is the completion of the surgery before the storm has reached its peak, and in this you can help me.

HENRY. No, Victor. I will have no part of this.

VICTOR. Think, Henry, think! To have control of life and death. Perhaps to remove disease forever from the human frame. To insure eternally the existence of the greatest minds. To...

HENRY. Do you aspire then to be a god?

VICTOR. God?

HENRY. Yes.

VICTOR. That thought had never even occurred to me.

HENRY. What of the soul, Victor? The body is but the keeper of the soul and death releases it to heaven.

VICTOR. And proctors of this soul would have knowledge disregarded and truths pronounced miracles. Mysteries were made to be solved, my friend. You taught me that. And Henry, I would have to see this soul before I could include it in my studies. (*Thunder. Henry turns away.*) I am no atheist, no blasphemer, but merely a scientist desiring to understand the secrets of life and perhaps, therefore, of God.

HENRY. Prometheus.

VICTOR. What?

HENRY. Prometheus was punished by the gods for bringing fire down to man.

VICTOR. Prometheus was a fool. The gods were jealous, greedy and possessive.

HENRY. (*Smiles despite himself.*) You are convinced that you can do this thing?

VICTOR. Yes.

HENRY. Even if I believed what you have said and thought you could achieve... I am overwhelmed. I believe you to be a good man, a brilliant scientist, capable of anything, and yet... my God!... it is fascinating!

VICTOR. It is more than fascinaiting. It is true. Please, my friend, come with me. See the wonders of which I speak. Join me in this enterprise. If, on further study, you choose to disagree... well... that is up to you. Meanwhile, time is precious and there is much that must be done.

HENRY. Are you so certain, then, that I will join you?

VICTOR. I have no doubt. Henry. No doubt at all. (*He crosses to the doors.*) Come.

HENRY. (*Hesitates.*) He was bound to a rock, you know. Prometheus.

VICTOR. My dear old friend, perhaps together we shall release him. (*He opens the door.*) Come. (*Henry smiles, his curiosity overcoming his apprehension as he crosses up and out the door, followed by Victor, who closes it behind him as the lights fade. (MUSIC 4.)*

ACT I

SCENE 3

(MUSIC 4a. Capped by thunder.) The laboratory. Later that night.

The laboratory is the topmost room of an old stone tower of the chateau. It has not kept pace with the rest of the house and whatever has been done to it has been done alone by Victor.

The main entrance is a wooden door to a raised gallery which runs, curving, across the entire width of the stage to a flight of stairs which curve down into the rest of the room. There are two large, arched windows along the gallery and stairs. One unlit torch sits in an iron stanchion. Off to one side of the lower level is a work area with a desk that overflows with notes, books, and charts. The rest of the room is filled with an assortment of electrical and chemical apparatus. Under the gallery, a generator. Under the stairs, a primitive control panel. A table filled with multi-colored, bubbling vials. Two enormous dangerous-looking pieces of electrical machinery sit D.L. and D.R. There is a large operating table c. on which rests the recently delivered body, still dressed save for his shirt which has been ripped open for the surgery. Cable and wire run everywhere in a maze of interconnections. Primitive electrical lights have been installed in the room.

The thunderstorm continues to build outside, with rumblings of thunder and occasional flashes of lightning visible through the windows and skylight.

As lights come up, Victor and Henry are at work on the body.

HENRY. Victor, there is no basis for this procedure anywhere in modern science.

VICTOR. (*Intensely, as he sutures.*) No, there isn't. (*He finishes.*

21

Henry cuts the thread.) ... good. But that, to me, is the great challenge of the sciences; to go beyond what anyone has done before. (*He gathers up the instruments and moves them to the desk.*)

HENRY. (*Checking the body.*) The flesh seems slightly rigid.

VICTOR. (*Rushes back. Feels.*) It will be all right. (*Thunder.*) There is no time to lose. The storm will peak soon.

HENRY. Victor. What has the storm to do with all of this?

VICTOR. It will flood the stream and bring the dynamo up to the necessary speed to give the machinery sufficient power to reinforce the charges which will surround the body in the air.

HENRY. I still don't understand.

VICTOR. There is an order to the life of things, Henry. A chain of violent activity that can be animated by the proper means. (*Henry stares at him, confused.*) Are you not familiar with Sir Humphrey Davy's "On the Chemical Effects of Electricity"?

HENRY. Vaguely.

VICTOR. Have you read Erasmus Darwin's *Botanical Garden?*

HENRY. Well yes, but...

VICTOR. (*Getting a book from his desk.*) Read this, then.

HENRY. (*Reads.*) "The temporary motion of a paralytic limb is likewise caused by passing the electric shock through it; which would seem to indicate some analogy between the electric fluid and the nervous fluid, which is separated from the blood by the brain; and thence diffused along the nerves for the purpose of motion and sensation."

VICTOR. Do you see?

HENRY. No.

VICTOR. (*Crossing to the* D.L. *machine.*) If a minor shock produces convulsive movement, might not a greater shock produce... (*He turns it on.*) ... continued animation?

HENRY. Yes. Yes, of course.

VICTOR. (*Turns it off.*) Or?

HENRY. Or. (*He suddenly understands.*) Or, if carried to extremes, re-activate a dormant heart!

VICTOR. Who knows?

HENRY. My God! (*Thunder.*)

VICTOR. Perhaps it is everyman's God.

HENRY. Yes. It may be possible. It just may be! (*Thunder.*)

VICTOR. Quickly, Henry. Bring down the chains! (*MUSIC 5.*)

*(*Quickly, Henry. We've no time to lose*) (*They move to the control panels and activate some switches. Four large chains descend into the room, followed by an enormous conical device which stops directly over the table. Henry moves to the table.*)

HENRY. Shall I connect?

VICTOR. Yes! (*Henry begins to attach the chains to the corners of the tabletop. Victor rushes up the stairs and looks out the window.*) The stream is rushing from the storm. The wheel is turning well. We should have plenty of power. (*He rushes down and throws a switch, which opens up the skylight. There is a knocking at the door.*)

ELIZABETH. (*Off.*) Victor! Victor!

HENRY. Elizabeth!

VICTOR. Yes, Elizabeth. What is it?

ELIZABETH. (*Off.*) Victor, please! Open the door.

HENRY. Victor, we must stop!

VICTOR. No, it is too late for that. Attach the bands! (*Henry secures a large strap across the chest of the body.*)

ELIZABETH. (*Off.*) Victor, let me in!

VICTOR. I'm sorry, Elizabeth. I cannot.

ELIZABETH. Victor, please! (*Henry takes hold of some wires dangling from the cone and begins to attach them at the head.*)

VICTOR. The primary first. At the base of the brain.

ELIZABETH. (*Off.*) You have been here since you left last night. Have you lost all track of time?

VICTOR. (*To Henry.*) Now the other. (*He joins him at the table.*)

ELIZABETH. (*Off.*) Henry! Henry! Are you there? Henry! Speak to him, please. You promised my your help.

VICTOR. (*Moving to the bank of switches.*) Elizabeth, please. Leave us! (*The pounding stops. Thunder.*) Can you feel it, Henry? The excitement, the power? This is the supreme instant. The culmination of my work. We stand at the threshold of a new age of man. The dawn of a new species who will bless us as their creators. (*He moves to the control panel.*)

HENRY. Victor, I am not so certain that...

VICTOR. Begin the sequence, Henry, for the moment of truth is upon us. (*They begin to throw the switches. The machinery picks up speed, begins to throb and pulse. Some other switches, and the speed increases even more. Henry races about as the build continues. The two large*

*Alternate line. See note on special effects at back of playbook.

D.S. *machines join in, surging and pulsing with raw electricity.*)
Elevate it, Henry. Keep it close to the induction coil! (*MUSIC 6.*)

*(*Activate it, Henry. Keep a watch on the induction coil!*) (*Some more switches and the cone begins to activate, throbbing madly as it and the tabletop begin a slow ascent to the roof. The storm and the machinery continue to build. The table reaches the top and there is a deafening crack of thunder and a huge flash of lightning just outside the skylight, followed by a smaller flash down the length of the induction coil.*) Now! (*They shut it down. The table and cone descend quickly as the rest of the machinery winds to a halt and returns to its previous ambient state. Victor and Henry detach the chains and a few of the restraining straps. Victor checks the pulse.*) It's alive. There is a pulse, Henry! A pulse!

HENRY. My God! Victor! (*He bends to listen to the heart.*)

VICTOR. Alive!

HENRY. (*Still listening.*) It's weakening.

VICTOR. What?

HENRY. It's weakening! I can barely hear it!

VICTOR. Quickly, some power! (*They spring to the switches and activate them. The machines build quickly and, without monitoring and regulation, approach what seems to be a dangerous level.*) More, Henry! Live, damn you. Live!

HENRY. There is no more!

VICTOR. More! For God's sake, give it more! (*The* D.L. *machine emits an enormous spark. The others begin to smoke. Henry begins to shut them down.*)

HENRY. Victor, we can't. I... (*Victor stares at him, incredulous.*)

VICTOR. What are you doing? Are you mad? (*They struggle.*) We'll lose him! He needs more power! More... power!

HENRY. Victor! Victor! (*The struggle ceases. Victor rushes to the body, checks the pulse. Finds nothing. Moves away in defeat.*)

VICTOR. We were so close, Henry. (*Pause.*) That all that time and effort should result in total failure.

HENRY. No, Victor. At least you've learned your principles are sound.

VICTOR. Yes. Yes, that's true. It did live, Henry. If only for a moment, but it did live.

*Alternate line. See note on special effects at back of playbook.

HENRY. Victor, please. I'm afraid that what we sought to do is far beyond us still.

VICTOR. We must not let simple disappointment cloud our vision now. We heard the heartbeat, felt the pulse. We did it, Henry. We did it! We gave this being life!

HENRY. Perhaps, Victor, it is better that it end like this.

VICTOR. Whatever the problem, it can be amended. We must re-analyze, re-examine every facet of our procedure, every piece of equipment... (*He gets his notebook from the table.*)

HENRY. We will, Victor. We will. But first we must take some time to think about what all of this might mean.

VICTOR. Yes, of course. (*He moves to a piece of machinery.*)

HENRY. What are you doing?

VICTOR. A moment, Henry. I must determine the exact amount of power which...

HENRY. (*Taking off his apron.*) Victor. Elizabeth is right. We are both exhausted.

VICTOR. But Henry, I only want to...

HENRY. Victor! Please...

VICTOR. Yes. All right. Some rest. Perhaps some food. (*He crosses, taking off his apron. Henry moves onto the stairs, takes the torch, lights it.*)

HENRY. Come.

VICTOR. Elizabeth! I must attempt to amend myself to Elizabeth, mustn't I?

HENRY. Yes. I think we owe them all some explanation. Especially your father.

VICTOR. And believe me, this storm is nothing compared to what we can expect from him. (*He takes his coat and shuts down the few remaining switches. The skylight closes, and the lights and the generator go off. He crosses up to Henry.*)

HENRY. I'm sure. I'm afraid he'll think that I've gone crazy too. (*A look back into the room.*) I'm not too sure I haven't.

VICTOR. Well, steel yourself. And let us rejoin, at least for tonight, the current family of man. (*They laugh lightly and exit, Victor casting one last long look down into the room. Silence. The storm continues to build. Ominous shadows are cast about the room. Suddenly there is a clap of thunder and streak of lightning just outside the window. The storm grows louder. Another bolt of lightning and the machinery*

25

turns on to its ambient state. The chemicals begin to bubble. A third streak of lightning and the apparatus begins to pulse and build. A larger, closer bolt and the two D.S. *machines are brought to life. The hum and throbbing builds until it seems that it can go no faster. Electricity arcs and crackles through the air. The cone begins to throb and pulse. Faster and louder, faster and louder, until... (MUSIC 7.) An enormous bolt of lightning strikes the building and travels down the cone to the body, which is enveloped in a blinding light. The table glows red hot and smoke pours from underneath it. The machinery begins to subside. As it does, the body sits bolt upright with a deep horrendous scream, tearing away the remaining straps as it does so. The Creature sits for a moment, breathing deeply as it recovers from the violence of its birth. Slowly, he begins to examine his surroundings. He lowers himself off the table. He moves slowly and begins to explore the room, touching, bumping, feeling, smelling — exploring at once his own senses and the things around him. He is drawn to the control panel and reaches out to touch it. He pushes a switch and the cone and chains rise up and out of sight. Another switch and the* D.L. *piece of machinery begins to glow. He crosses down in fascination and reaches out. He throws a switch and a light comes on. He reverses it and a second light replaces the first. Again and the first light reappears. Again, and the second replaces it. Once more, and the lights begin to alternate by themselves. He reaches out to touch them and the machine emits an enormous electrical charge. He backs away in fear and turns toward the sound of approaching voices. Victor, from offstage:)* Hurry, Henry. We must check everything. There is no telling what kind of damage the strike has caused. *(Victor and Henry enter. The Creature turns to face them, confused and frightened.)* My God!

HENRY. Victor! *(The Creature takes a step forward, emitting a pathetic, strangled sound.)*

VICTOR. We have suceeded, Henry! Look! *(The room is illuminated by a flash of lightning. The Creature reacts with even greater confusion.)* The lightning! It must have struck the table!

HENRY. Yes, of course.

VICTOR. Our machinery could never have produced so great a charge.

HENRY. *(Quietly.)* The fire of Prometheus.

VICTOR. The direct strike is what made it come alive!

CREATURE. *(With great difficulty, the word barely understandable.)* A L I V E. .

VICTOR. It's trying to talk. Remarkable. Truly remarkable!

HENRY. Victor, we must consider that it may be in pain.

VICTOR. Nonsense. It's alive. That's all that matters.

HENRY. No, Victor. We cannot forget that it is human.

CREATURE. (*Clearer.*) HU-MAN.

VICTOR. It can talk! It's learning potential is enormous!

HENRY. Victor, I... What will we do with him?

VICTOR. Do with him?

HENRY. Yes. Had you not thought of that?

VICTOR. We must examine him completely. Every function. Every reflex. (*He claps his hands. The Creature spins toward the sound.*)

HENRY. Victor, no. Listen to me. We cannot just...

VICTOR. Incredible! (*He circles to the other side, claps his hands again. The Creature responds.*) Here. Give me that. (*He takes the torch from Henry and approaches the Creature, raising it to see him more clearly.*)

HENRY. Victor, stop! Think for a moment.

VICTOR. (*Approaching with the torch.*) The eyes, Henry. Look at the eyes. (*Cornered, terrified, the Creature lashes out.*)

HENRY. Victor, look out! (*MUSIC 8.*) (*Victor is sent sprawling to the floor. Henry grabs up the torch and uses it to hold the Creature at bay. The Creature backs away from the threatening flame. He bumps into a piece of machinery which sparks at the contact. He cries out and moves toward Henry, who uses the torch to defend himself.*) Back! Back!

VICTOR. Be careful, Henry. His strength is unbelievable! (*Henry tries to calm the Creature who, backing away, starts up the steps to the gallery.*)

HENRY. Back! Easy now. Easy. That's all right. Easy. Easy. (*The Creature finds his way blocked by the closed door. He lunges toward Henry, who defends himself with the torch. The Creature backs away and crashes out the window. Thunder. Henry rushes over and looks down after him. Victor comes up the stairs.*)

VICTOR. (*Grabbing the torch as he passes.*) Come, Henry. There is no time to lose. (*He exits.*)

HENRY. Victor! What have we done?

VICTOR. (*Off.*) Come on!

HENRY. Victor! (*He exits as the lights fade.*) (*MUSIC 9.*)

ACT I

Scene 4

A cottage. One week later. Night.
*A single room. Simply furnished. A solid door. Fireplace with
cooking pot and utensils. A cot. Wooden table and chairs. Some
open shelves containing jars, a few books, some clothing.*
*(MUSIC 9a.) DeLacey is illuminated by the firelight as he sits
on a bench and stirs a pot of food. We see that he is blind as he
reaches for a piece of wood and prods at the glowing embers.*

VICTOR. (*Voice-over.*) Henry and I searched everywhere for
the body of the being, but our efforts to recover him proved
futile and we assumed that he had landed in the stream and was
taken by the storm. It was not until much later that I learned
what really had occurred... (*The door slams open and the Creature
enters. DeLacey hears him, turns.*)
DeLACEY. Who's there? (*The Creature does not move.*) Is someone there? (*He rises, moves toward the door. The Creature moves,
makes some noise.*) Are you children here again? Please, do not do
this to me. I am blind and all alone. (*He takes another step. The
Creature moans, presses himself against the wall.*) Who are you?
Please answer me. Who are you?
CREATURE. (*With difficulty, struggling to remember the word.*)
Hu-man.
DeLACEY. Are you hurt? Is that why you are here? (*The
Creature moans again. DeLacey advances, hands outstretched, toward
the sound. The Creature raises his hand as if to strike.*)
CREATURE. A L I...V... (*DeLacey touches him, pulls back his
hand at the contact. The Creature does not move.*)
DeLACEY. Can you not speak? (*The Creature moans again.
DeLacey takes his arm.*) There, there. It's all right. No one will
hurt you here. You are very cold, my friend. And wet. Here.
Come with me. (*He tries to lead him to the fire. The Creature resists.*)
No, no. It's all right. Come along now. (*Slowly, he manages to coax
him to the bench.*) Sit down here and we'll warm you up. (*The
Creature does not move.*) Sit down. Don't you understand?
(*DeLacey places a hand on his shoulder and pushes him down onto the
bench.*) Sit. Yes!

28

CREATURE. Ssss-it.

DeLACEY. So, you can talk after all. (*He crosses around behind him and sits.*)

CREATURE. Ssss-it.

DeLACEY. Is there something wrong with your voice? What has happened to you? (*The Creature, confused, moans and shakes slightly.*) It's all right. No matter. Here, let's warm you up. (*He takes the Creature's arms and extends them toward the fire. The Creature, afraid of the flame, draws back.*) No, no. Here. (*He takes his hands again and slowly places them in front of the fire.*) Here. Just here. (*The Creature feels the warmth and reacts positively.*) Yes. Warm.

CREATURE. W A... R...

DeLACEY. Warm.

CREATURE. W A R M.

DeLACEY. Yes. Yes!

CREATURE. (*Reaching toward the food.*) WARM! (*He burns himself on the pot draws back, moans.*)

DeLACEY. What is it? Are you hungry?

CREATURE. HUN-GRY?

DeLACEY. Yes. Of course you are. (*He reaches out for a bowl.*)

CREATURE. Hungry. Hungry.

DeLACEY. (*As he ladles porridge into the bowl.*) You are very simple minded, my friend. I hope you don't mind a very simple supper.

CREATURE. Hungry. (*He hands the bowl to the Creature, who begins ravenously shoveling it into his mouth with his hands. DeLacey hears the slurping and reaches up to stop him.*)

DeLACEY. Wait. Wait a moment. There is a better way. Like this. (*He takes the bowl away, gets a spoon, uses it correctly.*) You see? Like this. (*He demonstrates again, then takes the Creature's hand and fits it around the spoon.*) Now you try. (*He leads the Creature's hand to the bowl and then to his mouth. He eats.*) Yes. Yes. Again. (*He repeats the action. This time, however, the spoon returns automatically to the bowl and then back to the mouth.*) Yes. That's it. (*The Creature finishes and holds the bowl out to DeLacey, who of course doesn't see it. After a moment, he moans and pushes the bowl into DeLacey's chest.*) More? You want more?

CREATURE. More? (*DeLacey takes the bowl, refills it.*) More. Warm. Hungry. (*DeLacey hands him the bowl. He eats, grins happily.*)

29

DeLACEY. You learn quickly, my friend. Very quickly indeed. Can you tell me what it was that happened to you? (*The Creature chortles with pleasure. DeLacey chuckles to himself, thinks for a moment.*) My name is DeLacey. Can you say that? De-Lacey.

CREATURE. D E - L A C E Y.

DeLACEY. Yes, DeLacey. Good!

CREATURE. De-Lacey. Good! (*He returns to his food. Finishes.*)

DeLACEY. Yes, yes. And who are you?

CREATURE. (*Holding out the bowl.*) Hungry. More!

DeLACEY. Yes. All right. (*He ladles out more porridge.*) I don't know what it was that happened to you, but I suspect you know much more than you remember now. (*He hands him the bowl.*) No matter. I shall teach it all to you again. Everything I can.

CREATURE. (*Looks up.*) Good. DeLacey. Good!

DeLACEY. I have been here alone for a very long time. No one bothers with me much because I am old and blind. Children come here sometimes and torment me. They can be so very, very cruel.

CREATURE. DeLacey. Good.

DeLACEY. You don't understand anything I'm saying, do you? (*The Creature looks at him quietly.*) You will. I will teach you. For whatever the reason, you have come to me and I am no longer here alone. (*MUSIC 10.*)

CREATURE. Alone?

DeLACEY. No, my friend. Not alone. Whoever you are, you will stay here and become my student. My student and my friend.

CREATURE. Friend? (*DeLacey reaches out, touches the Creature's face.*)

DeLACEY. Yes. Friend. (*The Creature thinks a moment, then reaches out and tentatively touches DeLacey's face.*)

CREATURE. Friend.

DeLACEY. Yes. Friend.

CREATURE. (*Joyous. Excited.*) FRIEND! (*He gently strokes DeLacey's face as the lights fade.*) (*MUSIC 10a.*)

ACT I

SCENE 5

The cottage. Exterior. Three months later. Evening.
The cottage has been pivoted to reveal its exterior and comes to
rest at an angle off to one side of a clearing in the woods.
As it does, the lights change to indicate a passage of time and the
following voice-over is heard. (MUSIC 10b.) During it, the
Creature and DeLacey take their places on a bench to the L. of
the cottage door. There are gardening tools attached to the walls
and there is a small thatched overhang above the door supported
by a single wooden post.

VICTOR. (*Voice-over.*) The next few months passed quickly.
Henry was persuaded to remain until the wedding and together
we returned to more abstract and scholary pursuits. He was
able to convince me that my work was, after all, better left undone. My creation, meanwhile, was progressing rapidly; his
faculties re-acquainting themselves with skills and knowledge
that they had previously possessed. This period, although
shortlived, would be the only time of calm and peace that he
would ever know... (*Lights come up full. The Creature holds a book,*
is reading.)
CREATURE. ...Therefore the Lord God said, behold, the
man has become as one of us, to know good and evil: and now,
lest he put forth his hand and take also of the tree of life, and
eat, and live for ever:
DeLACEY. Very good. Go on.
CREATURE. ...Therefore the Lord God sent him forth from
the garden of Eden to till the ground from whe... whe...
DeLACEY. Whence.
CREATURE. I know the word. I could not see.
DeLACEY. It must be getting dark. That's enough for today
then. (*The Creature closes the book, hands it to DeLacey.*)
CREATURE. Adam was alone?
DeLACEY. Yes. Adam was the first man. God created him
from dust. Then God created Eve to be Adam's companion.
CREATURE. Companion is the same as friend?

DeLACEY. Yes, that's right. Get some wood. Then we'll begin preparing supper. (*The Creature rises, starts around the cottage.*)

CREATURE. (*To himself.*) Companion—friend. (*He exits. DeLacey remains seated. After a moment, Metz and Schmidt enter through the woods, carrying burlap sacks.*)

METZ. There he is. Now just keep quiet, Peter. And do exactly what I told you.

SCHMIDT. I don't like this, Hans.

METZ. Quiet, Peter! (*Comes down a few steps. To DeLacey.*) Hello!

DeLACEY. Who's there?

METZ. Just two travelers, sir.

DeLACEY. My name is DeLacey. This is my cottage. Is there something I can do for you? (*He rises, steps forward. Metz moves in.*)

SCHMIDT. No. We were just...

METZ. (*To Schmidt.*) Ssssh! (*To DeLacey.*) Yes. Perhaps there is something you can do. (*As he speaks, he signals Schmidt to go into the cottage. Hesitantly, Schmidt complies.*) We are on our way to Carlstadt. I'm afraid we've gotten lost.

DeLACEY. Carlstadt? You are a very long way from there.

METZ. Yes. It would seem we missed a turn somewhere.

DeLACEY. From which direction have you come?

METZ. From a village just outside Geneva. Do you think that you can help us?

DeLACEY. Yes. You should be glad you found me when you did. Go back north on the main road and shortly you... (*Schmidt re-enters, his arms laden with DeLacey's things. He trips on the doorjamb and falls.*) What was that? (*He turns in the direction of the sound. Schmidt tries to gather up the fallen objects.*) What's happening?

METZ. Nothing. My friend just dropped something. (*DeLacey takes another step, kicks something, reaches down, feels it, recognizes it as his.*)

DeLACEY. These things are mine! (*Schmidt snatches the object away from him, continues to gather up the others.*)

SCHMIDT. Just borrowing a few things from you, old man. (*He carries the objects over to the bags.*)

DeLACEY. Please don't do this to me. Please.

METZ. Not being very neighborly now, are you? Come on,

32

Peter. Gather it up and let's be off. (*He crosses to the bags. DeLacey bends down, picks up a scarf as Schmidt crosses back to get it.*)
SCHMIDT. Give me that!
DeLACEY. No!
SCHMIDT. Give me that! (*DeLacey clutches it to him.*) Hans!
METZ. (*Crossing in.*) Oh come now, Peter. Surely you can't be afraid of him? He's just an old man. And blind at that. (*He crosses to DeLacey, yanks the scarf away.*) You want this, do you? Come get it then. (*DeLacey moves toward him.*)
SCHMIDT. Here, old man. Over here.
DeLACEY. Please. Stop this. Please!
METZ. (*Mimicking him.*) Please! Please! (*They laugh. Metz goes to DeLacey, flicks him with the scarf. Schmidt begins to strike at him with an old blanket. They circle, taunting him.*) Here it is, old man. Here it is. You can have it if you can get it.
SCHMIDT. Come on! Get it. Get it!
METZ. Almost. Almost. Here it is. (*DeLacey catches the scarf, begins to scream.*)
DeLACEY. Help. Help me. Help!
METZ. Quiet!
DeLACEY. Help me! Someone, please!
METZ. Quiet, I said! (*Metz wraps the scarf around his throat, begins to strangle him.*)
SCHMIDT. Hans!
DeLACEY. Help! Help!
METZ. QUIET! (*He tightens the scarf around his neck. DeLacey gasps, strangled, slides slowly to the ground, still. The Creature enters around the side of the cottage, carrying a bundle of wood. Sees them, stops.*)
SCHMIDT. Oh my God. (*Metz turns, sees the Creature.*)
CREATURE. What are you doing? (*He drops the wood and comes forward.*)
METZ. (*Backing away.*) There... there's been an accident. (*Schmidt takes a lantern; starts to move toward the Creature, who is moving to DeLacey.*)
SCHMIDT. I know him. I know him...
METZ. We were... coming through the woods. (*The Creature kneels beside the body.*) We... heard screams. We...
CREATURE. What is wrong with him? (*He reaches out, touches the body.*) DeLacey? (*He rocks the body gently.*) DeLacey? Can you

33

not speak to me? DeLacey? (*Schmidt continues moving down in fascination. The Creature touches the body again, sits back in fear and confusion.* (*Screams.*) NOOOOOOO! (*He rocks slowly as he screams. Schmidt raises the lantern, looks at him.*)

SCHMIDT. (*Horrorstruck.*) My God. I know you. Frankenstein... we... those bodies... Hans! (*He begins to back away. The Creature looks up at him.*)

METZ. What are you talking about?

CREATURE. What have you done to him?

SCHMIDT. You were dead...

CREATURE. Dead?

SCHMIDT. Frankenstein...

CREATURE. (*Rising.*) Frankenstein? (*He approaches slowly, backing Schmidt toward the cottage.*)

METZ. (*Terrified.*) Oh my God.

SCHMIDT. (*Dropping to his knees.*) Don't hurt me. Please. Please!

CREATURE. What is this Frankenstein?

SCHMIDT. Oh God. Please. Please! (*The Creature grabs him by the coat, lifts him up.*)

CREATURE. What is this Frankenstein?

METZ. Leave him alone!

SCHMIDT. (*Babbling.*) Oh, God. Please don't. Please, I...

CREATURE. Tell me!

METZ. Run, Peter! (*Schmidt breaks away, climbing up the chimney of the hut to the roof, kicking at the Creature as he does so. The Creature pursues him.*)

SCHMIDT. (*Ad lib.*) Stay away from me! Stay away! No! Don't!

CREATURE. (*Ad lib.*) What is this Frankenstein? Tell me! Tell me! (*Metz counters to the other side, yelling to his friend.*)

METZ. (*Ad lib.*) Run, Peter! Over here! I'll help you! Here! Here! (*Schmidt loses his balance and falls backward through the roof with the lantern.*) Peter! (*MUSIC 11.*) (*The Creature comes down and starts toward Metz, who pulls a knife and backs away. Inside the cottage, Schmidt tries to open the door, which has been blocked by the broken post outside the door.*)

SCHMIDT. (*Ad lib.*) Hans, the lantern! Fire! Fire! Help me! Help me!

34

METZ. (*Beckoning with the knife.*) Come on, you! Come on. Come on!

CREATURE. Why are you doing this? Why? (*Metz jams the knife into the Creature's stomach. He doubles over, almost falls. Metz runs past him and pulls a pitchfork from the wall, uses the handle in an attempt to open the blocked door. Inside, Schmidt continues screaming. The Creature pulls out the knife and once again starts toward Metz, who strikes at him with the handle of the pitchfork. The Creature recoils from the blows, then catches the handle and pulls. Metz is spun around as he holds onto the end. The Creature shoves the handle away and drives the tines into Metz, who doubles over with a scream and collapses to the ground. Smoke begins to pour from the cottage and flames can be seen inside. The Creature, confused and in pain, looks around and then starts back toward the body. Schmidt can be seen inside the cottage, pounding vainly on the window.*) Why? Why? (*The fire is beginning to consume the cottage, the crackling of the flames growing louder and louder. Schmidt disappears. The Creature kneels beside the body, touches it, cries out in anger, pain and confusion.*) Friend! (*The sound of the fire continues to build as the lights fade.*)

CURTAIN (*MUSIC 12.*)

(*MUSIC 13.*) ACT II

Half-light. A clearing in the woods. Mid-day.
(*MUSIC 13a.*) *William and Justine are seated on the ground,
the remnants of a picnic strewn about. They are feeding Fritz,
laughing at his antics as he tries to get the pieces of food.*

VICTOR. (*Voice-over.*) The winter passed before I knew it as I
became caught up completely in the lives of those I loved.
WILLIAM. (*Holding up a piece of food.*) Get it, Fritz! Come on!
(*Fritz jumps up, gets the food.*) That's a boy! (*William looks around
for other scraps.*)
JUSTINE. That's all now, William. I think he's had enough.
(*William holds up another scrap.*)
WILLIAM. Come on, Fritz! Get it! Get it! (*Fritz gets it.*)
JUSTINE. William?
WILLIAM. All right.
JUSTINE. Now gather up your things and we'll be off. (*They
begin repacking the hamper. Fritz, unseen, wanders off.*)
VICTOR. (*Voice-over.*) William was fast becoming a young
man with a mind of his own, much to Justine's consternation.
She seemed to want to keep him always as the child that she
loved so much. Elizabeth and you, Father, were busy planning
for our wedding and Clerval proved himself to be the trusted
friend I remembered from the university. (*William yawns, tries to
stifle it.*)
JUSTINE. William. Was that a yawn?
WILLIAM. No.
JUSTINE. Do you think it's time to take a nap?
WILLIAM. Nooo! (*Looks around.*) Where's Fritz?
JUSTINE. I don't know. He must've wandered off somewhere.
He'll find us soon enough when he discovers that we've gone.
WILLIAM. (*Calls.*) Fritz!
JUSTINE. (*Calls.*) Fritz! (*They remain a moment, waiting.*)

VICTOR. (*Voice-over.*) I could not imagine then how our lives would be affected by the unholy thing that I had done.

WILLIAM. Fritz! We're going now!

JUSTINE. Perhaps he's gone into the barn. Why don't we go and take a look? (*William smiles. They start out.*)

WILLIAM. All right. (*He yawns again.*)

JUSTINE. And then we'll talk a little more about that nap.

WILLIAM. Ohhh!

VICTOR. (*Voice-over.*) We were all to be affected. You, Justine, Clerval, Elizabeth. (*They are gone. The stage is empty.*) And, may God forgive me, William... (*MUSIC 13b.*) (*Lights come up full. After a moment, Fritz enters. He sniffs around, slowly making his way across the stage. Suddenly his attention is caught by something in the bushes. He rushes off. We hear him begin to bark. It grows louder, more violent, then turns to a whimper and finally one sharp yelp of pain. Silence. The Creature enters.*)

WILLIAM. (*Off.*) Fritz? Fritz? Here Fritz! (*William enters, starts as he sees the Creature.*) Oh! Hello. Have you seen Fritz?

CREATURE. Fritz?

WILLIAM. Yes. He was here just a little while ago.

CREATURE. I have seen no one.

WILLIAM. He must have come this way. Would you help me look for him, please?

CREATURE. Yes.

WILLIAM. Fritz! Heeeere, Fritz! Well, help me! Friiiiitz!

CREATURE. Friiiiitz!

WILLIAM. Heeeere, Fritz!

CREATURE. Heeeere, Fritz!

WILLIAM. I can't imagine where he's got to. And I must get back before Justine wakes up or I'll really be in trouble. (*He calls, jumping up and trying to see over the bushes as he does so. The Creature calls after him, imitating the call and the jump each time.*) Fritz!

CREATURE. Fritz!

WILLIAM. Fritz!

CREATURE. Fritz!

WILLIAM. Could you lift me up please? Maybe I can see him through the woods. (*The Creature crosses, lifts him.*) No. (*The Creature continues to hold him, enjoying it thoroughly.*) You can put me down now. Put me down! (*He begins to struggle.*) Put me down! PUT ME DOWN! (*The Creature puts him down. William moves a little distance away, turns, stares at him.*) Don't do that please.

CREATURE. You are very small.

WILLIAM. I'm not! I'm almost eight.

CREATURE. Who are you?

WILLIAM. My name's William. Who are you?

CREATURE. (*Pause.*) I do not know.

WILLIAM. (*Sits.*) Are you from the village?

CREATURE. (*Drops to his knees, sits next to William.*) No. People from the village scream and run away from me. I do not know why.

WILLIAM. Has something happened to you?

CREATURE. What do you mean?

WILLIAM. Your face. It's... ugly.

CREATURE. I am now as I have always been.

WILLIAM. I'm sorry. I didn't mean to hurt your feelings.

CREATURE. You did not hurt me.

WILLIAM. I'm glad. I like you.

CREATURE. I like you too. You treat me like a friend. (*He reaches out, touches William's face, then notices the locket which hangs about his neck.*) What is this?

WILLIAM. It's a locket. My mother gave it to me. It has her picture in it. Here, look. (*He opens the locket, shows it to the Creature.*) She was very beautiful, wasn't she? (*The Creature looks, smiles.*) She's dead.

CREATURE. Dead?

WILLIAM. Yes. I don't remember her much. But I remember when she gave me this. (*He closes the locket, rises, begins to move away.*) Fritz!

CREATURE. (*Reaches out, takes his hand.*) Stay with me. Be my friend.

WILLIAM. We can be friends. But first I have to find my dog. (*Calls.*) Fritz!

CREATURE. Your dog?

WILLIAM. Yes. Fritz. My dog.

CREATURE. You did not say he was a dog. (*Rises.*) I know where he is!

WILLIAM. Why didn't you say so?

CREATURE. (*Happy, excited.*) Stay! Stay here! (*He disappears into the woods. William waits. After a moment, he re-appears, carrying the body of Fritz.*) (*MUSIC 14.*) Here! Here he is!

WILLIAM. (*Quietly, in shock.*) He's dead. (*The Creature kneels, places the body on the ground.*)

CREATURE. Fritz!

WILLIAM. (*His terror mounting.*) He's dead. Dead. Fritz. Fritz!

CREATURE. No. Please. Don't (*He reaches out to William.*)

WILLIAM. Don't touch me! Don't touch me!

CREATURE. Please... don't...

WILLIAM. (*Beating on his chest.*) You killed him! You killed him! Justine! Help! Help! (*The Creature grabs him, lifts him up into the air. William screams.*)

CREATURE. Do not scream! Please! (*In his confusion, the Creature hugs William to him, envelops him in his arms. William's muffled screams continue.*) Stop! Please! (*He squeezes him again and again. The screams stop, the body goes limp. Pleased, the Creature holds him out to talk to him.*) William. (*There is something wrong.*) William? (*He lays him on the ground, shakes him.*) William? Wake up, William. Please. (*He places Fritz's body next to William.*) Fritz! (*Looks at them. Thinks.*) Fritz is dead. (*He shakes William's body.*) William. Dead. (*He pulls the locket off.*) Mother. Dead. (*Thinks. Remembers.*) DeLacey. Dead. They called me dead. (*Confused, frightened.*) I am not dead. (*He looks at the bodies again. Reflects upon himself. Tensely, fiercely.*) I AM NOT DEAD! (*He sits back, reaches down to William as the lights fade.*) (*MUSIC 15.*)

ACT II

Scene 2

The sitting room. Two hours later.
(*Music 15a.*) *The room is empty for a long moment. Suddenly, the* U.L. *French doors fly open and the Creature stands framed in them. He enters and walks slowly about the room. He sees the mirror above the mantle. He approaches slowly and stares at it in wonder, never having seen himself before. He extends his hand and touches it, becomes disturbed at the realization of what he sees and tries to wipe the image away.* (*MUSIC 15b.*)

VICTOR. (*Off.*) Elizabeth? (*The Creature turns toward the sound.*) Elizabeth? (*He enters.*) Elizabeth? Are you... my God. You! You have survived. It isn't possible. We searched all along the river bank. Everywhere. We...

CREATURE. I... remember... you.

VICTOR. You can talk! (*Pause.*) How did you get here?

CREATURE. Frankenstein. I would know of Frankenstein.

VICTOR. What do you want of him?

CREATURE. Him?

VICTOR. I... am Victor Frankenstein.

CREATURE. (*Astonished.*) Frankenstein... you. (*Pause.*) Who am I?

VICTOR. (*The truth.*) I do not know.

CREATURE. They spoke as if you did.

VICTOR. Who?

CREATURE. Two men. They said your name. They said that I was... dead. They hurt me.

VICTOR. My God. Metz and Schmidt. You must leave this place for now.

CREATURE. No. I will not leave.

VICTOR. (*Placatingly.*) But you must understand. There are others here. If they should see you...

CREATURE. Yes. I am ugly. But I am also... (*A threat.*) ... strong.

VICTOR. All right. I will tell you what I can, but only in exchange.

CREATURE. No. You will tell me what you know.

VICTOR. I will, in due time. First I must find out...

CREATURE. Tell me now! I have thoughts I do not understand.

VICTOR. (*Carefully.*) You seek information here. I shall tell you. But I must know more. You must answer my questions. Do you understand? (*The Creature indicates that he does.*) Now then, tell me everything you can about the men who saw you.

CREATURE. They hurt me. They called me dead. And the others, they...

VICTOR. Others saw you?

CREATURE. Yes. They scream and run from me in fear. I...

VICTOR. Where did all this happen?

CREATURE. I am not as other men. I have memories... pain.

VICTOR. The people hurt you?

CREATURE. Yes.

VICTOR. Tell me exactly what it was that happened.

CREATURE. I have feelings that I do not under...

VICTOR. Where were you when you met these men?

CREATURE. I have feelings... pain... (*He touches his head.*) ... here...

VICTOR. When they said my name, did they...

CREATURE. (*Touching the area over his heart.*) ... and here. I...

VICTOR. Answer me. What...

CREATURE. I...

VICTOR. Answer me!

CREATURE. I... No more!

VICTOR. (*Trying to calm him.*) You must understand that...

CREATURE. (*Approaching.*) I understand nothing. You can tell me. (*He places his hand on Victor's shoulder, drives him to his knees.*) Tell me now! (*He throws him forward to the ground. Victor rises and moves away, cautioned by the Creature's sudden outburst of anger and enormous strength.*)

VICTOR. Very well. Ask your questions.

CREATURE. I have but one. What do you know of me?

VICTOR. Nothing. I...

CREATURE. (*Advancing angrily.*) Do not lie to me, Frankenstein! What are you to me?

VICTOR. I am... your creator! (*The Creature stops, stunned.*) You, that is your body, was at one time dead.

CREATURE. Dead. Creator.

VICTOR. Yes. I needed materials for my work and...

CREATURE. In the book of God...

VICTOR. You know the bible?

CREATURE. I know of the Creator. You are my Creator, and thus... (*Arms outstretched, He drops to his knees.*) ... my God!

VICTOR. No. I am not God.

CREATURE. You are my Creator.

VICTOR. I am not a god!

CREATURE. God is the Creator.

VICTOR. Yes. But there is only one God. I am not God!

CREATURE. Did you not create me?

VICTOR. Yes. No! I do not have power over life and death. No, I...

CREATURE. (*Rises.*) Did you then lie to me?

VICTOR. No! I...

CREATURE. Creator... God!

VICTOR. No! I am not...

ELIZABETH. (*Off.*) Oh, Father, you must have left them in the parlour. I'll get them and meet you in the garden.

VICTOR. Elizabeth! Quickly. You must hide. (*The Creature does not move.*) Hurry! Make no sound. (*The Creature crosses to the doors.*) Quickly! Or I will tell you nothing more!

CREATURE. I will wait. (*He exits, closing the doors. Victor barely crosses away as Elizabeth enters wearing a hat and shawl.*)

ELIZABETH. Oh, Victor. Here you are.

VICTOR. Yes. Is it time for William's lesson?

ELIZABETH. Oh! William and Justine are on a picnic.

VICTOR. A picnic?

ELIZABETH. Yes. Are you very angry?

VICTOR. No, of course not.

ELIZABETH. Good. Have you seen father's glasses?

VICTOR. No, I haven't (*He turns away as he starts to speak. As he does, Elizabeth crosses up to the French doors.*) As a matter of fact, I was very busy here and had quite forgotten William's lesson. I... (*He turns, sees her about to open the doors.*) Elizabeth... DON'T! (*She turns, startled.*)

ELIZABETH. Victor?

VICTOR. There is a draft.

ELIZABETH. (*Opens the doors.*) Don't be silly. (*He rushes to her side.*) There, you see? Not even the slightest breeze. What's the matter? I know something is the matter.

VICTOR. (*Leading her away.*) Nothing, Elizabeth. I swear. It's just that... (*Alphonse enters through the main doors.*)

ALPHONSE. Elizabeth! I had them with me all the time. Oh, Victor. Why don't you come along with us?

VICTOR. Where are you going?

ALPHONSE. (*Crossing to the French doors.*) We're going to look for William and Justine. They... (*He sees something.*)

VICTOR. (*Rushing up.*) What is it, Father? Do you see something?

ALPHONSE. Yes... I caught a glimpse of Mueller coming up the hill. Excuse me, won't you? (*He exits. Elizabeth crosses up to Victor at the doors. After a moment, the Creature appears at the other set of French doors. Listens.*)

ELIZABETH. Why don't you come with us, Victor? The air will do you good.

VICTOR. I can't just now. Perhaps later. Yes. I'll finish here and join you later.

ELIZABETH. Very well, my love. Don't be long.

VICTOR. No, I won't.

ELIZABETH. And Victor, please don't be angry about William's lesson.

VICTOR. No. Of course not. Goodbye. (*They kiss lightly and she exits. As Victor closes the doors, The Creature opens his and steps into the room.*)

CREATURE. Creator.

VICTOR. (*Spins at the sound.*) Leave here. Now! I have told you what you wanted.

CREATURE. No. There is more. I listened. She thought that you were angry. But you were afraid. Afraid she would see me.

VICTOR. And what of that? You are, by admission, hideous and ugly. (*The Creature grabs him around the head, covering his eyes.*)

CREATURE. Thus do I relieve you of my ugliness. (*He releases him. Victor drops to the floor, scrambles away, rises slowly, holding his head.*) I am alone in the world of man, where each and everyone shall hate me. (*He looks to the door where Elizabeth exited. Turns back.*) But you can change that, oh Creator. You must make another being... such as I.

VICTOR. (*Draws back.*) My God. No! Impossible!

CREATURE. Am I then, impossible? Oh my Creator, make me happy. The two of us shall leave the world of man and spend our lives alone together. You cannot refuse me this.

VICTOR. I do refuse!

CREATURE. (*Intense. Earnest.*) I will tell you something I have learned from man: he fears death above all else.

VICTOR. How do you know that?

CREATURE. I have been hated and hunted and I find no love in humankind.

VICTOR. You have killed!

CREATURE. Yes. A child. I did not mean to but he screamed like all the others.

VICTOR. Oh my God. What have you done?

CREATURE. What have we done, oh Creator?

VICTOR. (*Rushing to him.*) I am not responsible for you!

CREATURE. (*Grabbing him, holding him by the shoulders.*) Will you give me what I ask?

VICTOR. NO! (*The Creature throws him to the sofa, stands over him.*)

CREATURE. Listen to me. (*Pause. Steadily, purposefully.*) I took a chain that the child had been wearing. Later on I found a woman resting in a barn. Her beauty touched me and I was moved to leave it with her as a gift. But I can get it back from her just as I got it from the child. Do you understand?

VICTOR. Yes. (*Pause.*) I will do as you demand.

CREATURE. Tomorrow, then. We shall begin. (*He crosses to the door. Turns back.*) Do not betray me, oh Creator. For we are bound by ties that can never be undone. (*He exits.*)

VICTOR. (*Quietly, to himself.*) Except by death.

HENRY. (*Off.*) Victor? Victor? (*He enters, obviously upset.*)

VICTOR. What is it?

HENRY. (*Crosses in.*) Victor. Oh my friend.

VICTOR. What is it, Henry?

HENRY. (*Kneels next to him.*) William. William is dead, Victor. Murdered. He... (*Victor jumps up, stares in the direction of the Creature. Turns to Henry, shaken, despondent.*) Victor, please. Is there something I can do?

VICTOR. No. Nothing can help me now, Henry. Nothing. I have killed my brother.

44

HENRY. Victor, I know the shock is great; but to blame yourself for such an act, I...

VICTOR. It is true, Henry. It is true. I am responsible.

HENRY. But how could you be responsible?

VICTOR. Listen to me, Henry. Listen. That being we created? That thing that ran from here that night? It has survived!

HENRY. No. Impossible, Victor.

VICTOR. I have seen him, Henry. Here, today, within this very room. It is he who has killed William!

HENRY. How can you be sure?

VICTOR. He told me, Henry. He told me!

HENRY. We are, then, the both of us, responsible for his death. (*There is a knock on the door. Henry and Victor look at each other, wondering if they were overheard. The knock comes again.*) Yes. Who is it?

MUELLER. (*Off.*) It is I, Herr Mueller.

HENRY. Victor, say nothing until we have had time to think. (*Victor nods, tries to compose himself. Henry crosses to the door, opens it.*) Please. Come in, sir. (*Mueller enters.*)

MUELLER. I am sorry to intrude at such a moment. I would not have bothered you were it not of the utmost importance.

VICTOR. Yes. I know that.

MUELLER. I wish that I could simply offer my condolences, but I regret that I am here in my official capacity. Since your father has taken to his bed, I've asked Elizabeth to join us here.

VICTOR. Elizabeth! She must not be involved in this. She must not know what has occurred.

MUELLER. She already knows what has occurred.

VICTOR. No! She...

HENRY. (*Going to him.*) Victor! Calm yourself, please. Herr Mueller, please forgive him. He learned of William's death only moments ago and is understandably distraught.

MUELLER. Yes, of course. But you must also understand, I have my job to do. I believe that we have apprehended William's murderer.

VICTOR. What? Where did you find him?

MUELLER. Find who, Herr Victor?

HENRY. (*Covering.*) Who is it? Who have you arrested?

MUELLER. I'm sorry, I cannot say that yet.

45

VICTOR. Why are you doing this to me? Why?

MUELLER. Victor, you are acting very strangely.

HENRY. Herr Mueller, please. Think about what's happened here and you will understand the strain. (*Elizabeth enters. Victor rushes up and embraces her. Mueller crosses to the door.*)

VICTOR. Elizabeth, are you all right?

ELIZABETH. Yes.

MUELLER. (*At the door.*) Send her in. (*Justine enters. She has obviously been crying. Elizabeth goes to her, they embrace. Mueller crosses down, takes something from his pocket.*)

MUELLER. Elizabeth?

ELIZABETH. Yes? (*She crosses to him.*)

MUELLER. (*Holding out the locket.*) Do you recognize this?

ELIZABETH. (*With difficulty.*) Yes. That was William's. He wore it always for it contains a picture of his mother.

VICTOR. Where did you get that? Where?

MUELLER. We found it on the person of the murderer. Its presence makes it certain she is guilty.

JUSTINE. (*Shocked, on the edge of hysteria.*) I don't know anything about it. I swear. I would never have hurt William. Never! (*She begins to sob. They all stare at her in disbelief.*)

ELIZABETH. Justine? No, No. (*She goes to her.*)

VICTOR. (*Approaching.*) Fool! Madman! It was not Justine who murdered William! It was...

HENRY. (*Catching him.*) Victor!

VICTOR. ... Not Justine. (*He moves away. Elizabeth leads Justine to the sofa, sits her down.*)

ELIZABETH. Hush now, Justine. Hush. It will be all right.

JUSTINE. Oh, Miss. Please. You know that I could not have done what he has said. I loved William, Miss. I could never have done anything to... (*She breaks down.*)

HENRY. This is impossible. She is incapable of having harmed the boy. She is like a member of the family. She...

MUELLER. I understand your feelings, Herr Clerval, but this would not be the first time a servant has turned against a member of a family. A locket such as this would bring a good price in certain circles.

ELIZABETH. Justine. Justine, please. Tell me everything that happened. Please.

JUSTINE. (*With difficulty.*) William and I were on a picnic.

We sought the barn to take a nap. I was next awakened by Herr Mueller and his men. That is all I know. (*She breaks down again. Elizabeth comforts her.*)

MUELLER. We found the locket hidden in her skirt.

HENRY. Surely that is not enough!

MUELLER. I think that they will find it sufficient to convict her. And if they do, I'm afraid that she will be condemned. (*They look at him in horror.*)

ELIZABETH. No, no. Impossible. You cannot think that she would ever have harmed William. She...

HENRY. (*Overlap.*) Herr Mueller... Please. Can you not just wait a...

MUELLER. (*Overlap.*) I am sorry to have to do this, but I have no other choice. (*He crosses to Justine, takes her by the arm.*) Come along.

ELIZABETH. No, no. Please...

HENRY. Herr Mueller! (*Justine breaks away, runs to Victor.*)

JUSTINE. No! No! Victor, please! Help me! You must know that I am innocent. I could not have injured William! You cannot believe that I am guilty! Please, Victor. Say something! (*Mueller crosses over, takes her, leads her out.*)

MUELLER. Come along.

JUSTINE. (*As she exits.*) Victor! Help me. Please! Do not let them do this. Victor! Victor! (*She begins to sob as Mueller takes her from the room. Victor stands staring down. Elizabeth watches him, incredulous.*)

VICTOR. Elizabeth. I am sorry. I am sorry.

ELIZABETH. (*Slowly crossing down to him.*) How could you have let that happen? Why didn't you say something? Try to stop him from...

VICTOR. Justine is innocent. Of that I can assure you.

ELIZABETH. (*Grabbing him, forcing him to look at her.*) Of course she is! But it remains for us to prove her innocence!

VICTOR. (*At the edge of self-control.*) We cannot, Elizabeth. We cannot. And if she is condemned, I shall be forced to admit my...

HENRY. (*Rushing down. Stopping him.*) Victor! (*He steps between them. Gently.*) Elizabeth, please...(*Victor moves past them, heading up toward the French doors.*)

VICTOR. Only I can end this now. Only I. I must begin. (*He

47

opens the door and exits, closing it behind him. Elizabeth moves up, calls after him.)

ELIZABETH. Victor! (*She collapses onto the sofa. Henry goes to her, reaches out as the lights fade.*) (*MUSIC 16.*)

ACT II

Scene 3

(*MUSIC 16a.*) *The Laboratory. Two weeks later. Late afternoon. A storm is building.*
Victor is at work on the head of a sheet-covered body at the table. The Creature stands opposite him, watching intently. Near them is a smaller table with trays of instruments and beakers filled with milky liquids and indistinct objects. Victor selects an instrument and fits it into the Creature's hand.

CREATURE. What do you do now?

VICTOR. I am attempting to connect the muscles of the eye. (*Pause.*) This large nerve... here... carries the image from the eye to the brain. These large muscles... here... control the movement of the eye itself within the socket. The smaller ones control the focus. (*He removes something from one of the beakers slowly, with utmost delicacy and care, inserts it into the head.*) Careful. Now, release it. Slowly... slowly... good. (*He takes the instrument from the Creature, sets is aside, and lays strips of chemically treated bandages across the "eyes" of the body.*)

CREATURE. Why do you do that?

VICTOR. The eyes must be protected from too sudden an exposure to the light. Please ask no more questions. The work is difficult enough without...

CREATURE. I ask questions of you that I may learn.

VICTOR. Daily do I bring you books. I have, of necessity, taught you something of the sciences so that you could assist me in this endeavor. (*With building anger.*) You speak, you see, you breathe, you move, you think! You have taken the life of my brother! What more is there that you can ask of me?

48

CREATURE. There is much to ask of you, oh Creator, as any child asks of its parent.

VICTOR. Enough! No more talk. There is work that must be done.

CREATURE. But I must know more if I...

VICTOR. I say no! We have a bargain. I will keep it. But I am master here! (*Pause. Victor returns to work.*)

CREATURE. Why this work?

VICTOR. Because you have forced me to it.

CREATURE. No. Why me? Why did you do this to me? Why did you create a being that even you turn away from in disgust? (*Victor does not respond.*) I have read your notes while here alone. I read of potions, solutions, incisions, but I find nothing that will tell me why. I am most confused.

VICTOR. You are damned! (*Thunder.*)

CREATURE. If I am damned for being alive, how damned are those that brought about my being?

VICTOR. There will be no more talk. I want you out of my sight and out of the lives of those I love. I cannot finish here soon enough to suit me for then I will be rid of both you and your despicable companion.

CREATURE. I will hear no more of this!

VICTOR. Do you threaten me again? (*He looks at the body on the table.*) It grows tiresome.

CREATURE. (*Bested.*) We have made a bargain. I will honor it. (*Thunder. Victor looks up.*)

VICTOR. We must make sure that everything is working before the storm begins to reach its peak. (*He moves to the switches, points to the D.L. machine.*) Throw that lever when I tell you. (*The Creature moves to the machine.*) Now! (*They throw the switches and the machinery starts up.*) Now the other. (*He moves about, checking everything.*) And the next. Now! (*There is a pounding on the door.*)

HENRY. (*Off.*) Victor! Open this door! Victor... damn you man. I know you're in there. (*Victor rushes about, shutting everything down. The Creature spins toward him in confusion and disappointment.*)

VICTOR. Here... quickly, hide yourself.

HENRY. I will not leave until you let me in!

VICTOR. (*Covering the body with the sheet.*) A moment, Henry, for God's sake! (*To the Creature.*) Hurry! I shall deal with this as quickly as I can and then we will get back to work. (*The Creature hides behind the* D.L. *machine. Victor starts up the stairs.*)

HENRY. Victor!

VICTOR. A moment, Henry! (*Victor lifts the latch and throws open the door. Henry enters, outraged.*) Good God, Henry, how dare you...

HENRY. How dare I? Victor, I am appalled by...

VICTOR. Leave here immediately.

HENRY. Why are you here? Why were you not with your family when they had need of you?

VICTOR. What are you talking about?

HENRY. Justine is dead! (*Thunder.*) Dead, Victor.

VICTOR. What? Justine... oh my God... today.

HENRY. Yes, today! She is dead. Hanged by the neck in the public square.

VICTOR. No.

HENRY. Yes! Ah, but of course, you weren't there. (*Victor moves away. Henry pursues him.*) She was driven to the gallows in a wooden cart.

VICTOR. Henry, please...

HENRY. She was drawn through the assembled crowd. They spit on her and called her filthy names. Her face was very pale. She was frightened and alone. Yet she managed to maintain dignity.

VICTOR. Henry, stop...

HENRY. Then she saw Elizabeth. Justine cried out. Elizabeth broke from the crowd and started running toward the cart. She was restrained and stopped by the gallant Herr Mueller. She screamed Justine's name and Justine cried back to her, calling over and over until the rope tightened about her neck and silenced her forever. (*Pause.*) Where were you, Victor? What kind of a man are you? I do not know you anymore. (*He turns away.*)

VICTOR. But we agreed, Henry. Discussed it and agreed that there was nothing we could do in light of her confession.

HENRY. You know as well as I that she confessed out of fear for her immortal soul. There was something that we could have done! We... (*He suddenly becomes aware of his surroundings.*) Why

50

are you here? What are you doing? God damn you, Victor! What are you doing?

VICTOR. (*Pushing him toward the stairs.*) Leave, Henry. Leave before it is too late. For your own sake, Henry, leave me!

HENRY. What are you doing? What?

VICTOR. I have no choice, Henry. (*He turns away.*) I cannot break my promise.

HENRY. Promise? What... (*He sees the body, mistakes it for the Creature.*) Oh my God. I understand. No, Victor. No. You need not do this thing alone.

VICTOR. Henry! Please. You do not understand.

HENRY. Oh, but I do. Victor. I do. You have lured him here somehow and are planning to destroy him. Oh, my friend, forgive me for misjudging you.

VICTOR. No, Henry! No!

HENRY. There is no reason to proceed in this alone. Together we created him and together we will bring him to an end. (*He turns, takes off his coat.*)

VICTOR. Henry! You do not know what you are doing!

HENRY. (*Hangs up his coat, takes an apron, turns back.*) Quickly, Victor. We must not waste any more... (*Thunder. The Creature steps out.*) (*Dumbfounded.*) You! I...

CREATURE. Do you propose to stop the work that has begun? Do you dare to make him break his promise?

HENRY. Promise? (*To Victor.*) What filthy promise have you made?

CREATURE. I have been alone. He is making my companion.

HENRY. Companion! (*He drops the apron, rushes to the table, looks. Crosses back.*) No, Victor. No! It is impossible, unthinkable to even dream of creating another being such as he.

VICTOR. I must, Henry. I must. For only then will he depart and leave us all in peace. I have his word.

HENRY. His word!

CREATURE. Yes.

HENRY. But what of this thing you are creating? It may be ten times worse than its intended mate.

CREATURE. I have sworn to go away.

HENRY. You may have sworn, but that has not! (*To Victor.*)

What assurance do you have that that thing will comply with his conditions?

CREATURE. I have promised!

VICTOR. She will obey him, Henry. She must. I can see to that. (*He crosses to the* D.L. *machine, turns it on. It glows steadily. Henry pursues him.*)

HENRY. No, Victor, no. You cannot continue in this vile, thoughtless act.

CREATURE. (*Angry.*) I have endured pain, and misery, and loneliness. Shall each man find a wife and each beast a mate, and I be alone?

HENRY. (*Summons up his courage, approaches.*) There can never be another thing like you.

CREATURE. I cannot reason with you, for you prove yourself unworthy. (*He turns slightly away, thinks. Turns back.*) You are my creators; but I am master here. Obey, or you shall know the power of my hate.

HENRY. (*Frightened; determined.*) No. I will not waver before your threats. (*The Creature lunges out and hurls him against the* D.L. *machine, which springs to life* (*MUSIC 17.*) *at the contact and emits an enormous electrical charge. Henry's body shakes violently and almost seems to glow as the current surges through it.*)

VICTOR. HENRYYYYYY! (*He rushes to the control panel and throws a switch, shutting down the machine. Henry's body is released and crumples to the floor. Victor stares at him, then screams.*) Noooooooo! (*He grabs a mallet from the panel and slams it repeatedly into the body of the female, destroying it. The creature bellows in anguish and rage. A final blow, and Victor crosses down to face him.*) Now kill me and have done! (*The Creature grabs him and hurls him to the floor, rushes down, arm raised, looms over him, beside himself with rage. Stops.*)

CREATURE. No. (*A deadly intensity.*) Shall you find release in death while I remain desolate and alive? (*Anger building, he goes up the stairs onto the gallery.*) You have destroyed my dreams and hopes of peace. (*He looks down at the body of the female with great sorrow, then looks slowly back at Victor.*) But hear me and remember well: I SHALL BE WITH YOU ON YOUR WEDDING NIGHT! (*Thunder. Flashes of lightning silhouetting the Creature against the window.*)

Blackout (*MUSIC 18.*)

52

ACT II

SCENE 4

(MUSIC 18a.) Elizabeth's bedroom. One year later. Late afternoon.

The room is beautifully but simply furnished. The entire U.S. *wall is covered by an enormous tapestry.* D.R. *is a large free-standing chifferobe. Up of it, a canopied bed.* U.L., *double doors to the rest of the house.* L. *of* C., *a dressing table and chair, and* D.L., *a free-standing full length mirror.*

Lights come up slowly during the voice-over to reveal Elizabeth seated at the dressing table and Frau Mueller working on her hair. (MUSIC 18b.)

VICTOR. (*Voice-over.*) Nearly a year has passed since the day he murdered Henry and his trail has lead me north throughout all Europe to this land of endless, barren ice. I shall close this journal and come home now, Father, as I lost sight of him some weeks ago and feel convinced he must have perished in the cold. Though I shall never know for certain and the memory of his existence will remain to haunt my life forever... (*Lights up full.*)

FRAU M. There. Oh, you look lovely, my dear. Such a beautiful bride.

ELIZABETH. (*Rises, looks at herself in the mirror.*) It was Madame Frankenstein's dress, you know.

FRAU M. Yes. She wanted you to wear it on your wedding day.

ELIZABETH. Well, I could not be happier than to be reminded of her.

FRAU M. Oh, if only she could be here now. (*Elizabeth sits, Frau M. crosses behind her.*)

ELIZABETH. Have you seen Victor yet?

FRAU M. No. Not since early in the morning.

ELIZABETH. Isn't he with Father and the guests?

FRAU M. Lionel told me that he was there for a while, but then it seems he disappeared.

ELIZABETH. Disappeared?

FRAU M. Yes. They said that he was acting rather strangely.

ELIZABETH. Frau Mueller, please.

FRAU M. Now, Elizabeth. You yourself have told me that since he returned from his year of travels in the north, his moods have been just filled with ups and downs.

ELIZABETH. Yes, they have. But how could they be otherwise with everything that's happened?

FRAU M. Of course, my dear. I'm sure that you are right. But to act so strangely...

ELIZABETH. Frau Mueller, today is his wedding day.

FRAU M. Well yes, but...

ELIZABETH. And just how calm was Lionel prior to his marriage?

FRAU M. Not calm at all.

ELIZABETH. You see?

FRAU M. Of course. (*They laugh.*) Now, is there anything else, Elizabeth?

ELIZABETH. I don't think so.

FRAU M. Then I shall go and tell them you are ready!

ELIZABETH. Thank you. (*Frau M. starts out. Elizabeth stands, looks in the mirror.*) Frau Mueller!

FRAU M. (*Turns.*) Yes?

ELIZABETH. My veil! (*They both smile at this obvious omission.*)

FRAU M. It must still be in the closet. (*Frau M. crosses to the chifferobe. Just as she is about to open the doors...*)

ELIZABETH. Frau Mueller, does everyone feel like this on their wedding day?

FRAU M. Yes, my dear. Of course they do.

ELIZABETH. (*Turning to her.*) I do hope everything will be all right.

FRAU M. (*Crossing to her.*) Elizabeth, everything will be just perfect. Now, let me get your veil. (*She crosses back to the chifferobe. Victor enters.*)

ELIZABETH. Victor! What are you doing here?

FRAU M. (*Crossing up.*) Victor, really. You should not be here, you know.

VICTOR. Yes, I know. Would you excuse us for a moment, Frau Mueller?

FRAU M. Well, all right. But don't be long.

VICTOR. I promise.

FRAU M. Really! (*She exits, smiling and shaking her head.*)

ELIZABETH. Really, Victor. You should not be here. It is

bad luck, you know.

VICTOR. How very beautiful you are. (*They kiss.*) Bad luck indeed.

ELIZABETH. They do say that, you know.

VICTOR. Who?

ELIZABETH. Oh... I don't know. (*She smiles.*)

VICTOR. I love you, Elizabeth.

ELIZABETH. And I love you.

VICTOR. Do you really?

ELIZABETH. Yes. Oh, yes. And with every day I love you more. (*Victor moves away, glancing nervously about the room.*) Is something wrong?

VICTOR. No, Elizabeth. No. Indeed not.

ELIZABETH. Are you sure?

VICTOR. Yes. Of course I am. I...

ELIZABETH. Oh be happy, Victor! I will not allow you to distress yourself on this most happy night.

VICTOR. This night! Oh, that this night had long since passed!

ELIZABETH. Victor, why do you speak like that? Something is wrong.

VICTOR. (*Trying to cover.*) No. That is, I...

ELIZABETH. What is it?

VICTOR. Elizabeth, there is something you must know.

ELIZABETH. What?

VICTOR. I... this is most difficult. I...

ELIZABETH. Tell me, Victor. Please.

VICTOR. My experiments, Elizabeth!

ELIZABETH. No. Do not torment yourself like this. It has been a year since the accident with Henry. You...

VICTOR. (*Grabs her, stares.*) Listen to me, Elizabeth!

ELIZABETH. (*A little frightened by his intensity.*) Yes?

VICTOR. (*Faltering. With difficulty.*) I... I don't know where to start. (*Moves away.*) You see, I was fascinated by the power and the secrets of electricity and began to wonder about the very origins of life. I...

ELIZABETH. Victor, please. I have heard all this before!

VICTOR. (*Rushing up, grabbing her by the arms.*) No, Elizabeth. You have not. (*Quiet. Intense.*) I discovered principles that I carried to extremes.

ELIZABETH. Extremes? What sort of extremes?

VICTOR. I conceived of the idea and executed the creation of a man!

ELIZABETH. (*Pulls away. Shock, disbelief.*) A man?

VICTOR. Yes, a man! (*It all pours out.*) A creature, hideous and deformed and perverse beyond imagining. It was he who murdered William and Clerval. He who placed the locket which condemned her in the folds of Justine's skirt. And he who swore to be with me this very night! (*Elizabeth moves away, leans on the dressing table, her back to Victor, who counters* D.R.) I know what you must think of me, but I could no longer bear the guilt. I had to tell you, even though I knew that I would lose you too. (*Elizabeth turns, looks at him. Crosses to him.*)

ELIZABETH. No, Victor, No. There is nothing that could destroy the love I feel for you.

VICTOR. Elizabeth. (*He clutches her to him.*)

ELIZABETH. Hush, my love. Calm yourself. For we are to be married soon.

VICTOR. (*As if struck.*) Elizabeth! We must get away from here tonight!

ELIZABETH. Yes. We'd always planned to...

VICTOR. No! We mustn't even wait for that! We must leave immediately after we are married.

ELIZABETH. But the guests, they...

VICTOR. (*Crosses to the door.*) I don't care a thing about the guests! I only care that you and I, together, are well away from here. (*Turns to her.*) Tell me it's all right?

ELIZABETH. Yes, of course. (*She moves toward him. His mood becomes ecstatic and he sweeps her up into his arms.*)

VICTOR. Elizabeth!

ELIZABETH. (*Laughing.*) Victor!

VICTOR. Oh, Elizabeth. I love you so. (*They kiss. Deeply. Elizabeth finally breaks it.*)

ELIZABETH. Victor, please. I have to finish packing.

VICTOR. What?

ELIZABETH. Packing . . .

VICTOR. Oh. Yes. Of course. I'll help you. (*He crosses to the chifferobe, reaches for the doors, turns back.*) Tell me what you need. (*Alphonse enters.*)

ALPHONSE. Ah, there you are. I've been looking all over for

you. The guests have wondered at your absence. They... is something wrong?

ELIZABETH. No, Father. We simply sought to escape for a moment.

VICTOR. We had some things to talk about. Certain memories to overcome.

ALPHONSE. Yes, I know. But we cannot dwell in the melancholy past. Soon new and dear objects of affection shall be born to replace those of whom we have been so cruelly deprived.

VICTOR. You're right, Father. (*Looking at Elizabeth.*) The future is the only thing that matters now.

ALPHONSE. Come, the two of you. The guests are waiting. It is time. (*He starts out. Victor and Elizabeth draw together and kiss. Alphonse turns back, sees them.*) Come along, now. Plenty of time for all that. (*He exits. Victor swings Elizabeth around and they start out. Just as they reach the door, Elizabeth stops.*)

ELIZABETH. Victor! I've nearly gone without my veil!

ALPHONSE. (*Off.*) Victor?

VICTOR. Yes, Father. (*They exchange a look and Victor exits. Elizabeth crosses back into the room and goes directly to the chifferobe. She stops, reaches out, pulls open both the doors — and removes her veil. She closes the doors, turns and, as she starts to go, (MUSIC 19.) the tapestry on the back wall is torn away revealing the Creature standing in an alcove. Elizabeth spins and gasps in fear. She backs up against the chifferobe as the Creature steps down into the room.*)

CREATURE. I am here for retribution.

ELIZABETH. No. I...

CREATURE. (*Moving toward the doors.*) I have been betrayed and he shall suffer for the injuries inflicted.

ELIZABETH. (*Moving toward him.*) No. Do not harm him. Please. (*She kneels.*) I beg you. (*The Creature stops.*)

CREATURE. I shall not harm him... in the way that you think. (*He starts to turn toward her.*)

ELIZABETH. Then why are you... (*Their eyes meet. He approaches slowly.*)

CREATURE. You shall be the instrument of my revenge. Your screams shall summon him here and he shall see that I have kept my word. (*He reaches out, touches her hair.*) I wish I did

57

not have to harm you... (*She recoils from his touch.*) ...but I have no other choice.

ELIZABETH. (*Trying to overcome her revulsion.*) No. Please. I... (*The Creature takes her by the arms, lifts her up, stares into her face.*)

CREATURE. So scream, Elizabeth. Scream.

ELIZABETH. No. (*He grabs her by the back of the neck, thrusts her toward the door.*)

CREATURE. Scream. Scream! (*She bites down on her hand to keep from screaming. The Creature grabs her by the wrist, whips her around, squeezes her arm, forces her to her knees.*) Please. Please! Scream!

ELIZABETH. (*Summoning her strength, rises up. Gasping.*) No. (*He takes her by the shoulders, throws her onto the bed. She rolls, gets up, backs away against the headboard. The Creature draws himself up, approaches slowly.*)

CREATURE. You will give me my revenge.

ELIZABETH. No. (*He grabes her round the throat, pushes her down onto the bed, strangles her. She struggles, gasps for breath. He bears down. As her arms go limp and she dies, he screams...*)

CREATURE. Frankenstein! (*He stumbles up into the alcove, bellows at the top of his voice.*) FRANKENSTEIN!

VICTOR. (*Off.*) (*Approaching.*) Elizabeth? Elizabeth! (*He bursts into the room carring a pistol and is overcome by the scene which confronts him: Elizabeth's body hanging from the bed, her arms outflung, her eyes open and staring.*) Oh my God. (*He sees the Creature.*) NOOOOO! (*He raises the pistol and fires as the Creature exits. He starts after him.*)

Blackout (*MUSIC 20.*)

ACT II

Scene 5

(*MUSIC 20a.*) *The Laboratory. Immediately following. The room is empty. Victor and Alphonse enter. Victor carries the torch and the pistol. They stand on the gallery and look down into the room.*

ALPHONSE. Victor, what are we doing here? (*MUSIC 20b.*)
VICTOR. A moment, Father. Here. (*He hands Alphonse the pistol and starts down the stairs. Stops to place the torch in its stanchion.*)
ALPHONSE. Mueller and the others are searching the grounds. Come, we'll join them there. (*Victor crosses into the room, checks the hiding place behind the* D.L. *machine.*)
VICTOR. No. It is here that he will come. Of that you can be certain. (*Alphonse crosses down, begins to look around.*)
ALPHONSE. My God, Victor. What is all of this?
VICTOR. Over, Father. All of this will soon be over.
ALPHONSE. (*Crossing* D.C.) What have you to do with this?
VICTOR. (*Crossing down to join him. As he speaks, the Creature enters through a trap* U.S.C., *directly behind them.*) Father, you will find a journal in my bureau. It will explain everything that has occurred.
ALPHONSE. But what do you...
VICTOR. Please, Father. We must prepare for his arrival. (*The Creature slams the trap. Alphonse and Victor turn at the sound.*)
ALPHONSE. (*Horrorstruck.*) My God!
VICTOR. Shoot him, Father.
ALPHONSE. I... I...
VICTOR. Shoot him! (*Alphonse raises the pistol. The Creature grabs his arm, pulls the pistol from him, pushes him violently away.*) Father! (*He rushes in. The Creature turns. Victor backs away. The Creature throws the gun* U.)
CREATURE. If it is revenge you seek, Frankenstein, it would be better served in my life than in my death.
VICTOR. Accursed thing! You have murdered the helpless and the innocent who never injured you or any other living thing.
CREATURE. Do you think her death has brought me

pleasure? (*He turns away.*) My crimes have degraded me beneath the meanest animal. Even my revenge has left me with a bitter taste.

VICTOR. And I? Do you think that I am free of guilt? Of pain? Of responsibility?

CREATURE. (*Turns back. Quietly. Simply.*) No. For it was you who gave me life.

VICTOR. Yes! (*He dives for the gun, raises it and fires at the Creature, who approaches as the bullets strike him. He grabs Victor's wrist. The gun drops. Victor screams. The Creature lifts him up across his back, places his hands over his legs and chest. Victor screams and struggles as the Creature bends him slowly backwards across his shoulders until Victor's back breaks with an audible crack. He hangs limply across the Creature's back until he shrugs him off onto the ground. The Creature looks at him a moment, then kneels beside the body.*)

CREATURE. Farewell, Frankenstein. I have destroyed you and everything you ever loved. I shall die as you are dead who called me into being and, when we are gone, the memory of us both shall quickly vanish. But we will at last be bound together, forever all alone. (*He rises and crosses to the bank of switches.*) And thus the instruments of life become the instruments of death. (*One by one, he switches them on. The machinery starts up, begins to build. He crosses back, kneels, cradles Victor's body in his arms. The machinery begins to spark and smoke. He looks around slowly and then shouts with great joy and resignation:*) FAREWELL! (*The machinery begins exploding. Flames lick up and the lab begins to crumble. Some more explosions and it falls in upon itself, the Creature and his Creator. Lights fade.*)

CURTAIN. (*MUSIC 22.*)

(*MUSIC 23.*)

PRODUCTION NOTES

While *Frankenstein's* production requirements are certainly more complex than those of the average "straight" play, they are actually less demanding than a number of musicals which are commonly performed at the amateur and collegiate level. A "non-musical musical" is the way that we approached it in New York and while the Broadway production certainly took full advantage of its spectacular possibilities, it has also been produced with great success in regional theater, colleges and summer stock with substantially reduced physical values.

SCENERY

It is unlikely that *Frankenstein* will ever be done as a "black box" play, but that is not to say that it cannot be done on a relatively simple scale. For example:

The *Graveyard* (Act I, Scene i) and The *Forest* (Act II, Scene i) can be played without any scenery at all other than a mound of dirt for the one and a picnic blanket for the other.

The *Sitting Room* (Act I, Scene ii; Act II, Scene ii) requires the furniture, the French windows, a door and a fireplace. Connecting walls can easily be eliminated and replaced by drapes for masking.

The *Bedroom* (Act II, Scene iv) can use the same French Windows (*covered by the tapestry*) and door. (As a matter of fact, this is exactly what was done on Broadway). Replace the fireplace with the bed and chifferobe.

The *Cottage* (Act I, Scenes iv & v) needs nothing more than the three walls with door, either free-standing or mounted on a wagon. Between scenes, simply pivot them to reveal the exterior.

The *Laboratory* (Act I, Scene iii; Act II, Scenes iii & v) is the centerpiece as far as scenery is concerned. If you have a question as to where to spend your money, spend it there. Bear in mind that whatever machinery and equipment it contains has been installed and built by Victor Frankenstein himself. There is no reason why it cannot look homemade. Obviously, though, the more flashing lights, etc., the better. By the way, a "Jacob's ladder" can be easily constructed from some copper rods and a neon transformer (ask a local electrician). In the original St. Louis production all the cables, wires and connectors were left exposed. It looked terrific, adding to the overall sense of clutter and "electricity," made internal sense—the machines did have to be connected, after all—and at the same time provided all the "dressing" that was needed. Bottles filled with colored water and hooked up to an aquarium airator made the chemicals. The operating table was little more than an old piece of iron grating salvaged from a junk yard and mounted on a base. Other than that, it only needs the back wall, window and the staircase.

SPECIAL EFFECTS

Although the various effects are an integral part of the production, it is also conceivable that, in some instances, the play itself could easily be overwhelmed by them. You can afford to be selective. Specific effects done well will be more effective than all of the effects attempted and done badly. Use your imagination. The following will show you some alternatives that do work:

Act I, Prologue.
Victor can stand alone in a spotlight in front of the act curtain which is bathed in the revolving light of a mirrored ball to represent the snow.

Act I, Scene i—The *Graveyard*
Dry ice fog. Low light. Henry's arrival in the carriage can happen off stage.

Act I, Scene ii—The *Parlour*
The approaching thunder storm and lightning. The storm is on tape; the bank of strip lights (*upstage of the French windows*) flashing at the appropriate moments give the effect of lightning.

Act I, Scene iii—The *Lab*
A continuation of the "storm" throughout. Flashing lights in

the machinery, pulsing faster as they "build". If the body cannot be elevated, the line on P. 22:

VICTOR. Quickly, Henry. Bring down the chains.

can be replaced by:

VICTOR. Quickly, Henry. We've no time to lose.

and the line on P. 24:

VICTOR. Elevate it, Henry. Keep it close to the induction coil!

can be replaced by:

VICTOR. Activate it, Henry. Keep a watch on the induction coil!

The creation itself is a modulated build of all the machinery as before, capped by an enormous bolt of lightning (sound and strip lights). Some bright light on or around the body and, if possible, a flash and/or smoke pot underneath the body tops it nicely, followed by another clap of thunder (sound) and lightning (strip lights) outside the window just after the Creature sits up.

The breakaway window for the Creature's fall can be replaced by a breakaway curtain or by nothing at all. Seeing him unexpectedly disappear through the opening is startling enough.

Act I, Scene v — *DeLacey's cottage, exterior.*

A ladder attached to the hut and a breakaway roof (if you feel adventurous) or simply having the actor playing Schmidt go over the back of the roof or the wall into a stack of mattresses are two alternate approaches to the fall. Some smoke from the inside of the hut and flickering red light (accompanied by the sound of flames) give a very nice illusion of the fire.

Act II, Scene iii — The *Lab.*

The machinery and storm are as before. The female Creature

need never be seen and her death can be done by hiding blood packs underneath the sheet that covers her. Henry's death can be effected by two or three flash and/or smoke pots hidden in a piece of machinery which ignite at the instant that he makes contact. Dimming all the stage lights at the same moment adds to the idea of a "power drain."

Act II, Scene iv — *Elizabeth's Bedroom*

No effects, although the reveal of The Creature behind the tapestry is the biggest scream in the show. The tapestry must be large enough for the audience to believe it is the "back wall" of the set. The shock is totally dependent on the "false" crosses to the chifferobe and the audience's belief that is where The Creature is. You'll find the proper timing the first time you have an audience. The gunshot should be done live if possible.

Act II, Scene v — The *Lab*.

The destruction can be accomplished by the use of flashpots, smoke, flickering colored lights and the appropriate accompanying sound. At the very end, almost simultaneous with the curtain, a few chunks of painted styrofoam thrown from the wings or dropped from the flies add greatly to the illusion.

SOUND

I cannot stress enough how effective and important the use of sound can be to the success of a show like *Frankenstein*. It helps enormously in establishing atmosphere and place, even more so, in some cases, than your scenery. Howling wind in Act I Prologue; softer wind in the Graveyard; the storm throughout the Parlour and The Lab. The sounds of the machinery which can automatically convey a sense of "build." Light forest sounds underneath the picnic. Some music from "downstairs" underneath the Bedroom scene. More wind throughout the final Lab. The sounds of explosions and destruction.

Don't be afraid of using music in between the scenes. It helps to cover set changes and also provides emotional transitions. Richard Peaslee's score for Broadway approached it much the way he would a film. I strongly recommend its use.

MAKE-UP

Stitches, scars, the pallor of the dead. Avoid the flat-topped square head and bolts in the neck of the movies. In the first place, it's copyrighted by Universal Films but, even more than that, it invites unnecessary comparisons to the classic Boris Karloff interpretation of The Creature.

A final word:

Frankenstein is meant to be a fairy tale. It is the novel approached through the memory of the films. It is meant to be played "straight," not as a modern play, but as a Victorian one. It is meant first and foremost to entertain and to engage the imagination. It is a story, not a "theme," and if you tell the story well, then whatever else it has to say will undoubtedly be heard.

Victor Gialanella
October 13, 1981

PROPERTY PLOT

ACT I, Scene i (The Graveyard)
Shovel
Pickaxe
Body (In shroud)
Burlap
Lantern (Metz)
Lantern (Victor)
Lantern (Henry)
Coin (Henry)

ACT I, Scene ii (The Parlour)
Book (Elizabeth)
Embroidery (Justine)
Locket (William)
Glasses (4 Brandy, 2 Sherry)
Decanters: (1 Brandy, 1 Sherry)

FURNITURE:
Armchair
Sidechairs (2)
Endtables (2)
Sideboard
Settee
Fireplace with tools and mirror above
Frankenstein family crest

ACT I, Scene iii (The Laboratory)
Suture (Victor)
Tray with instruments: (Scalpels,
  Forceps, Probes, Clamps, etc.)
Books: (Medical texts, Journal)
Charts
Notes
Jars w/chemicals
Torch (In wall stanchion)
Lab aprons (Victor, Henry)

FURNITURE:
Operating table
Wooden work bench
Chemical area

ACT I, Scene iv (The Cottage)
Cast iron pot w/food
Bowl
Spoon
Ladle
Poker
Firewood

FURNITURE:
Bed
Table
Bench
Shelves (w/Clothes, Old Books, Pot-
  tery, Plates, Glasses, Pot and pans)

ACT I, Scene v (Outside The Cottage)
Bible (Creature)
Lap robe (DeLacey)
Lantern (Schmidt)
Empty burlap bags (Metz and
  Schmidt)
Bench
Knife (Metz)
Pitchfork (On side of Cottage)
Stolen goods (Schmidt): Plates, Pots,
  Scarf, Assorted clothes, Glasses,
  etc.)
Old blanket (Schmidt)
Firewood (Creature-off)

ACT II, Scene i (The Forest)
Book (Justine)
Picnic Blanket
Plates (2)
Glasses (2)
Food scraps (Practical for Fritz)
Toy soldiers (William)
Cake
Napkins
Picnic basket
Fruit

Utensils
Dead dog (Creature-off)
Locket (William)

ACT II, Scene ii (The Parlour)
Schoolbook (Victor)
Shawl (Elizabeth)
Hat (Elizabeth)
Gloves (Elizabeth)
Book (Alphonse)
Glasses (Alphonse)
Locket (Mueller)

FURNITURE:
Same as ACT I, Scene ii (Strike liquor and glasses)

ACT II, Scene iii (The Laboratory)
Clamp (Creature)
Scalpel (Victor)
Forceps (Victor)
"Eye muscles" (Implanted by Victor)
Gauze strips
Salve
Sheet (Covering Female Creature)

Mallet
Lab aprons (Victor, Henry)

ACT II, Scene iv (The Bedroom)
Hand mirror
Comb
Brush
Hairpins
Hair combs
Wedding veil (In chifferobe)
Gun (Victor-practical)

FURNITURE:
Dressing table and chair
Bed
Chifferobe (Dressed w/hanging clothes, shoes, etc.)
Tapestry (As large as possible, covering the French doors from ACT I, Scene ii)

ACT II, Scene v (The Laboratory)
Torch (Victor)
Gun (Victor-practical)

Costume Note:

Without detailing the many changes used on Broadway (and they can be as many or as few as your budget will allow) there are a few items that are more important than others. While working in the lab, Victor and Henry should remove their coats and work in shirtsleeves and leather aprons, which are kept on hooks attached to the set.

The Creature may either wear an operating gown or first appear on the table partially dressed (shoes, pants, an open shirt.) He can acquire an outer garment (or, indeed, all his clothes) between ACT I, Scene iv and ACT I, Scene v. This may be changed for a different one (given him by Victor?) between ACT II, Scene ii and ACT II, Scene iii.

The same rule of selective priority applies to the costumes as it does to the sets and special effects. One basic suit for the men may be modified considerably by a different shirt or tie, as can the women's clothes be affected by a shawl (for Elizabeth) or an apron (for Justine). Mueller can wear somethng which suggests a "uniform" throughout and neither the Graverobbers nor DeLacey need to change at all. A real "Wedding Dress", however, would seem to be a necessity for Elizabeth in ACT II, Scene iv. "Tails" for the men in the wedding scene but, if not, a black suit with dress shirt and bow tie will do.

MUSIC CUES

1. - ACT I Overture

1a - Prologue underscore. Fade to low level at curtain rise, continue under Victor's speech.

2. - Into Graveyard. On blackout.

2a - Fade out as dialogue begins.

3. - Out of Graveyard. On blackout.

3a - Into Sitting Room. Cross fade up as Music 3 is faded down and out. Then fade out as dialogue begins.

4 - Out of Sitting Room. As lights fade.

4a - Into Lab 1. As lab appears. Cap with thunder.

5. - Suspense underscoring. As chains are lowered. Continue until Music 6.

6. - Body Elevation underscoring. Fade as body is lowered.

7. - The Creation. As lightning strikes the body.

8. - Chase underscoring. As Victor is knocked to the floor. Continue until Music 9.

9. - Out of Lab 1. As lights fade.

9a - Into Cottage. Cross fade up as Music 9 is faded down and out. Then fade out just before The Creature opens the door.

10. - DeLacey's Theme. Fade up slowly on line ". . . and I am no longer here alone." Keep at low level under rest of scene.

10a - Fade up Music 10 as scene ends. Continue under scene change.

10b - Fade Music 10a down and out as Victor's voice-over begins.

11. - Fire Music. As Schmidt falls through roof. Continue slow fade up under rest of scene.

12. - ACT I Curtain. On curtain.

13. - ACT II Overture.

13a - Forest Music. On curtain. Establish, then fade down to low level. Continue under scene.

13b - Fade out music 13a.

14. - Heartbeats (Dead dog underscoring). As Creature re-enters carrying the body of the dog. Continue under rest of scene.

15. - Out of Forest. As lights fade.

15a - Into Sitting Room 2. Cross fade up as Music 15 is faded down and out.

15b - Fade out Music 15a on Victor's first offstage call: "Elizabeth?"

16. - Out of Sitting Room 2. As lights fade.

16a - Into Lab 2. Cross fade up as Music 16 is faded down and out. Then fade out as dialogue begins.

17. - Electrocution underscoring. As Henry is thrown against the machine.

18. - Out of Lab 2. On the blackout.

18a - Into Bedroom. Cross fade up as Music 18 is faded down and out.

18b - Fade down Music 18a under Victor's voice-over. Then fade out as dialogue begins. (Optional: Continue at very low level until Music 19 as if music were coming from "downstairs")

19. - Tapestry Sting. As the tapestry is ripped away.

20. - Out of Bedroom. On the blackout.

20a - Into Lab 3. Cross fade up as Music 20 is faded down and out.

20b - Fade out Music 20a as dialogue begins. (Optional: Continue at low level throughout scene until Music 21.)

21. - The Destruction. As the Creature activates the machinery. Start at low level and build until Music 22.

22. - ACT II Curtain.

23. - Curtain call and Playout.

Note: The above cues refer to the original score composed for *Frankenstein* by Richard Peaslee. Other sound effects (thunder, machines, explosions, etc.) may be taken from any standard sound effects recording. The music is not intended to replace them.